PRAISE FOR *TIPPING POINT*

My good friend and ministry partner Jimmy Evans has been studying biblical prophecy for 45 years. In his newest book, *Tipping Point,* he offers compelling evidence about the end times. I believe Jimmy's voice and perspective are critically important at this point and time in history.

Robert Morris
Founding Lead Senior Pastor, Gateway Church
Best-selling Author of *The Blessed Life*, *Beyond Blessed,* and *Take the Day Off*

Exploring the prophetic parts of Scripture can be tricky, and no one handles them with more care and insight than my friend Jimmy Evans. Drawn from years of thoughtful Bible study and meticulous historical research, *Tipping Point* shines like a beacon of light through the circumstantial darkness of worry, fear, anxiety, and uncertainty. If you want a greater understanding of prophecy in God's Word, then don't miss this book!

Chris Hodges
Senior Pastor, Church of the Highlands
Author of *The Daniel Dilemma* and *What's Next?*

The end times and prophecy are on the minds of believers everywhere, and there is no one better than Jimmy Evans to inform and instruct on what is next for God's people. He is a favorite of the *Joni Table Talk* viewers, and I am certain *Tipping Point* will answer many questions for those looking for the soon return of our Lord Jesus Christ!

Joni Lamb
Co-Founder, Daystar Television Network

To understand biblical prophecy is to understand heaven's perspective on earthly events. I know no one with the ability to do so like Jimmy Evans.

Tim Ross
Lead Pastor, Embassy City Church

Tipping Point is not your typical book about the end times. It is a wake-up call and an invitation to understand the times in which we live. Pastor Jimmy presents a convincing end times road map with revelation, wisdom, compassion, and comfort. His writing is insightful and engaging and leaves you excited to be part of a time like this. Be ready—Jesus is coming soon!

Luis Roman
Senior Pastor, VIVA Church International
XO Latino Host

Now, more than ever, the world needs hope. Hope is rooted in knowing that God is in control and that Jesus is coming again soon. Jimmy Evans offers a deeply biblical, well-researched, and incredibly powerful perspective on the end times that is critical to understand.

Rabbi Jason Sobel

Many believers find themselves frightened about biblical prophecy. However, approximately 30 percent of the Bible is prophetic in nature, and the study of prophecy is crucial for both instructing and comforting us that God is ultimately in control. In *Tipping Point,* Pastor Jimmy weaves together biblical truths and practical applications, making prophecy approachable and understandable.

Mark Driscoll
Founding Senior Pastor, The Trinity Church
President, Mark Driscoll Ministries
Author of *Win Your War* and *Spirit-Filled Jesus*

The first sermon I ever heard Jimmy Evans preach was on end times prophecy in the Bible. That was over 26 years ago! I was blown away that day by his deep understanding and fresh revelation of the connection between biblical prophecy and present day issues. He effortlessly connects 2,000-year-old biblical texts with today's headlines and points it all toward God's love for His people. Jimmy's passion for and understanding of biblical prophecy are second to none! I strongly endorse *Tipping Point,* and I encourage both the casually interested and the biblical scholar to dive in. Jesus is coming back. The time to get ready is now!

Jimmy Witcher
Senior Pastor, Trinity Fellowship Church

Pastor Jimmy has always had an incredible ability to bring understanding to complex subjects. If you are looking for clarity and hope for the quickly approaching end times, this book is for you.

Dr. Jon Chasteen

President, The King's University

Lead Pastor, Victory Church

Prophetic powerhouse Jimmy Evans deciphers the signs of our times and comes to the conclusion that this is the deep breath before the plunge. It's a glorious day to be alive. *Tipping Point* makes it clear that the supernatural romance between Jesus and His people is reaching a climax. The Bridegroom is at the door. I'm full of joyful anticipation after reading this book.

Troy Brewer

Senior Pastor, OpenDoor Church

Troy Brewer Ministries

FOREWORD BY **MAX LUCADO**

TIPPING POINT

THE END IS HERE

BESTSELLING AUTHOR

JIMMY EVANS

To the prophets of the Old and New Testaments who faithfully spoke and wrote what God said to them in the face of persecution and death. We have the light of Bible prophecy to guide us in these dark days because of your courage and obedience.

CONTENTS

FOREWORD

My dad made a big deal out of family vacations. He enjoyed preparing for a trip as much as the trip itself. Our vacations always consisted of a long road trip that began at our home in West Texas and ended up in a campground. Colorado was a favorite destination. He was even known to take us as far as Yellowstone or the Grand Canyon. Weeks before we left, he would start planning the route. He had no internet or GPS; he planned his trips the old-fashioned way. He used a map.

He would trace out the journey with a highlighter. He circled the campgrounds and made notes of the highway numbers. And once he had his plans, he shared them with us.

My brother and I were just kids, single digit in age and inexperienced in the ways of the road. So my dad would sit us at the table on the eve of departure and tell us what to expect.

When we drive through New Mexico, it's going to get windy.

When we reach the mountains, your ears will pop.

You'll know we are almost to the campground when you see snow on the mountain peaks.

He told us what to look for. And wouldn't you know it, he was right. The wind *did* blow. Our ears *did* pop. And the snowy peaks were the last thing we saw before we reached our destination.

My father told us what to expect.

Our heavenly Father has done the same.

Did you know that 30 percent of your Bible is prophecy? Entire volumes such as Isaiah, Ezekiel, Daniel, and Revelation are prophetic. To dismiss prophecy is to dismiss one-third of the Bible. Yet many people do. They do because prophecy can be complicated and teachers of prophecy can be opinionated. "Just give me Psalm 23 and the Lord's Prayer," some say. "I can make sense out of those passages."

Don't be among them. God will give you wisdom. He assures a special blessing to those who study and heed prophecy (see Revelation 1:3). He equips certain of His teachers with the ability to help the rest of us.

One of those teachers is my friend Jimmy Evans. He is passionate about helping us see the road that lies ahead. He has dedicated his adult life to studying the words of the prophets so you and I can have better understanding. I first heard the messages of this book in audio form when Pastor Evans presented them at Gateway Church. My wife and I listened carefully and intently to his teaching. I cannot tell you how many times I said to myself, "That makes perfect sense" or "I never thought of it that way." The teaching informed, inspired, and encouraged me.

To be clear, no one knows everything about the future. Any teacher who acts as if he does needs to be dismissed. Jimmy Evans approaches this topic with humility and reverence. We can be grateful for what he has done. We need this teaching today.

There is a story about an airplane lost over the ocean in the middle of a hurricane. The captain announced over the intercom, "I have good news and bad news. The bad news is, I have no idea where we are or where we are headed. The good news is, we are making great time."

That describes the lives of many people today. We are busy but lost—in a hurry with no destination. We run faster than ever, but we do not know where we are going.

But to all who will listen, God will share the destination. He opens the map and tells us where we are headed and what to look for.

Just like my dad. Why did he tell my brother and me what to expect? Why give us a heads up about windy weather, popping ears, and mountain peaks? I never asked him, so I can't say for sure. But here is what I think: he didn't want us to be caught off guard. Good dads protect their kids. He protected us from unnecessary fears.

Our good God is protecting us too. He gives us signs, not to make us anxious but to make us aware. And to help us prepare. From my perspective, we sure seem to be seeing a lot of snow-covered peaks. Our destination is closer than we've even imagined.

Max Lucado
Best-selling Author,
Teaching Minister, Oak Hills Church

ACKNOWLEDGMENTS

To my precious wife, Karen—Thank you for your unwavering love and encouragement. I would not be the man I am today without you.

To the elders, staff, and congregation of Gateway Church—I am privileged and proud to call you my church family. Your trust and support mean the world to me.

To my son, Brent—Thank you for your leadership, your creativity, and your commitment to excellence. You bring life to every project, and I am proud to work with you.

To Joni Smith, Chris Stetson, and the staff at MarriageToday™—Thank you for your hard work and consistent devotion. You truly are the greatest team!

To John Andersen—Thank you for working tirelessly to bring this book from its beginning stages to the finish line.

To Jenny Morgan—Thank you for your careful research and dedication to detail.

Finally, a special thank you to *Tipping Point Prophecy Update* newsletter subscribers. Your hunger for truth and passion for God's Word bring me great joy.

INTRODUCTION

I received Christ as Lord of my life in 1973 when I was 19 years old. One week later my wife, Karen, and I got married. We were both new believers, and we started attending church regularly as well as a young marrieds class. In that class, they challenged us to pray and read our Bibles daily. The only problem was I didn't own a Bible and didn't know one verse of Scripture.

The next week, Karen and I went to a local Christian bookstore so we could each purchase a Bible. I had never been in a Christian bookstore, so it was a new world for me. I had no idea they had so many different books on so many topics. As I browsed through the bookstore, I noticed a book by Hal Lindsay called *The Late Great Planet Earth*. I picked it up, studied the cover, and then looked at the table of contents to see what the different chapters were about.

After examining it for a few minutes, I realized I was holding a book that talked about the prophetic destiny of the world and what the Bible said about it. It was shocking to me that the Bible predicted future world events. I purchased the book, took it home, and read it immediately. I was completely fascinated by it. As I read what Hal Lindsay said about Bible prophecy, I looked up each Scripture to make sure it was in the Bible. It took me a while because I didn't know where any book or verse was.

In every case I found that the Bible said just what Lindsay claimed. And in the process I fell in love with the Bible and prophecy. That was almost 50 years ago, and since that time I have read hundreds of books on prophecy and studied every prophetic Scripture many times. I have also preached on Bible prophecy many times over the past 40 years and regularly appear on television programs to discuss prophecy and how it relates to current events in the world today.

As you will read in this book, I believe the end times officially began in 1948 when Israel became a nation in one day. That began the prophetic clock ticking. Since that time, we have seen prophecy after prophecy fulfilled, and they are still unfolding constantly around the world. There is virtually no mathematical chance that these events could be accidental. They are proof that there is a Master in charge of all things and that He controls the world and the future.

Even though that is all true, I have found over the years that some people don't like Bible prophecy. It actually frightens them to hear about the end times. I empathize with those people, but the truth is Bible prophecy was given to us to comfort us, not to frighten us. When you understand what the Bible says about the end times, you realize that we as believers are rescued from the horrific judgments of which the Bible speaks. We will not be here when those things happen because Jesus is returning to take us to be with Him forever. Also, when you understand prophecy you are able to contextualize the events that are happening in the world. While others are confused or frightened, you can be calm and comforted. This is especially true in times when we are experiencing pestilences like COVID-19 and other world events. It is one of the reasons I am so thankful for the gift of Bible prophecy.

In 2000 Malcolm Gladwell wrote *The Tipping Point: How Little Things Can Make a Big Difference.* In that book Gladwell discussed how ideas, products, and messages spread like viruses until no one can stop them. So, we have the same title, but we don't share the same subtitle or subject matter—not even close. However, when we use the term *tipping point,* we do mean the same thing. Gladwell defines *tipping point* as "the moment of critical mass, the threshold, the boiling point."[1]

You see, I believe we have reached the boiling point of something far bigger than a particular social or cultural change. I believe we have approached the biggest event in world history—the end of the age. In fact, I wouldn't even say we are approaching it; we are already there, and these things are happening *now.* Take a moment to let these next two sentences sink in. I don't only believe that end times events are happening right now. I believe we are living in *the end of the end times.* Take a deep breath. I'm not going to leave you there. I am going to show you the truth of what I am saying in the Scriptures. I am also going to show you how to have hope and peace in the midst of it all.

—————————•—————————

I DON'T ONLY BELIEVE
THAT END TIMES EVENTS
ARE HAPPENING RIGHT
NOW. I BELIEVE WE ARE
LIVING IN *THE END OF
THE END TIMES*.

The signs of the end times are all around us. We have reached a critical and unstoppable point so significant that nothing can be done by anyone or anything to keep it from happening. There is no going back. This is the world we are living in today, right now. We are at the tipping point, and the end is here!

Approximately 30 percent of the Bible is prophetic in nature? And most of the prophecies in the Bible are concerning the end times and our generation. You might wonder why the Bible would say so much about the final generation. I believe one of the main reasons is because more people are alive on the earth at this time than have ever lived at all times over the history of the world. I also believe there is another significant reason: this is the most severe time in human history. Jesus said, "In fact, unless that time of calamity is shortened, not a single person will survive. But it will be shortened for the sake of God's chosen ones" (Matthew 24:22 NLT). We are living in very serious times. God knows it, and for our sake, He has given us end times Bible prophecy to instruct us and comfort us.

There are many religions on the earth right now claiming that their god is the true god and their literature is divinely inspired. If that is the case, why can't their god or "sacred" literature predict the future with accuracy? I can tell you the answer: the only One who can foretell the future is the One who controls it. Our God is the only true God who controls all things. And for that reason we are the only people on the earth today who can truly say with confidence that we have empirical, measurable, definable proof that our God is real and our Bible is inspired by Him. And prophecy gives us that proof!

My prayer is that this book will educate, comfort, and inspire you. God bless you!

ISRAEL AT A
TIPPING POINT

1

THE BEAUTY OF
BIBLE PROPHECY

The Bible is beautiful. Have you ever thought about it in those terms? The more I have read it over the years, the more I can see just what an incredible masterpiece God has given to us. Yes, I believe the Bible is pure truth and contains no errors, but it is even more than that. It is like a priceless treasure, woven together by a master craftsman. Personally, it has captured my love and imagination, and I have dedicated my life to filling my heart and mind with its truth.

Recently, one of my friends told me about a professor he heard at The King's University talk about the "aesthetics" of the biblical story. This teacher was making a practical application about the beauty of the Christian story as an alternative to other stories the world might tell. In particular, he was saying one of the ways to witness and share the gospel with some of the people in the younger generations is to ask them to compare their "pictures" of the world with the story of what God has done through Jesus Christ—the Bible's worldview.

For example, which story is more beautiful?

- We live in a world with many beautiful things, yet much of it is desperately broken, including people. Nothing can be done about it, except to survive it and make it marginally better until we die. After that, there is nothing.

- We live in a beautiful world with many beautiful things, yet much of it is desperately broken, including people. However, we believe Someone created that beauty, and the brokenness is not His doing nor His intent. He intends good for both the world and the people in it. In fact, this Creator cared so much for His creation that He became one of us and took all the pain and brokenness on Himself, even to the point of dying for it. Even so, that did not end His story. He rose from the dead and is re-creating the world, beginning with those people who will love and follow Him. One day He will fix absolutely everything and restore the beauty with which the world began, and we will live and reign with Him for all eternity.

Now, I ask you again, *which is the better story?* Of course, you picked the second one. But even more than that, the second one is the truer story. *It is both more truthful and more beautiful.*

You see, God's story from beginning to end is the most beautiful thing you will ever hear, see, or read. On the other hand, our human story is ugly and extremely disappointing, if it weren't for the fact that God chose to become part of our story because of His great love. And so, I begin this book by telling you about the beauty of the Bible from beginning to end. Specifically, I want you to see the beauty of prophecy in the Bible as it applies to this book.

The Bible is not just one story that stands on equal footing with every other competing story. No, it is *the* story. When I say the Bible is a story, I don't mean to say it is fiction or a fairy tale. In a way the news it delivers seems so good that it's hard for some people to believe it. But I say to you, *believe it.* The Bible is as beautiful as it is true. It is God's continuing story, and for us, it is the only way our story has the happy ending God wanted for us all along.

FIVE TRUTHS ABOUT BIBLE PROPHECY

As I said in the introduction, the Bible's prophetic material distinguishes it from every other book in the world. Again, around 30 percent of the Bible contains prophecy, and most of the prophecies relate to the end times. Throughout this book I will remind you of some of the most important truths about Bible prophecy. If something is important, I will repeat it. Here are *five* of those truths to keep at the front of your mind:

1. *The only One who can predict the future with absolute certainty is the One who controls it* or someone who is a direct

representative of the one who controls it. God controls the future. Consequently, God's messages about the future are our only reliable source of truth about it.

2. *God gives us prophecy to warn unbelievers and comfort believers.* How do you respond when you hear the Bible's prophecies? If you are fearful then maybe you aren't ready for the return of the Lord, and you need to make some changes in your life. Or are you hopeful? Through a proper understanding of Bible prophesy, you lose all fear and dread of the end and instead look forward to it. That is the purpose of this book. I want you to truly understand end time prophecy so you can be comforted and be able to contextualize the events occurring in the world.

3. *Prophecy gives us the assurance that all the Bible is true.* The Bible tells the truth about the future. How do we know? Because many things the Bible tells us will happen have already happened. As God fulfills what the Bible foretells, we have concrete, measurable proof that the Bible and all its prophecies are true.

4. *The Bible and the Christian faith have no rival that can help us understand the future.* No other book in the world and no other religion can come close to predicting the future in advance the way the Bible has done. There is only one God, and His version of events is our only sure picture about what will happen in the future.

5. *Confirmation of the Bible's truth depends on the truth of its prophetic writings.* If those prophecies don't come true, then the credibility of the entire Bible is in jeopardy, including its claims about Jesus Christ. However, there is no mystery because the Bible's truth is easy to measure. We can know the accuracy of the Bible's prophecies because they are *incredibly specific.*

FIVE PROPHECIES REGARDING ISRAEL

When I say the Bible's prophecies are specific, allow me to supply some examples. The Bible gives us the conditions of the end times and specifically conditions related to Israel. It also tells us all these conditions will occur within a single generation. Consider Jesus' words in Matthew's gospel:

> Now learn this parable from the fig tree: When its branch has already become tender and puts forth leaves, you know that summer *is* near. So you also, when you see all these things, know that it is near—at the doors! Assuredly, I say to you, this generation will by no means pass away till all these things take place (Matthew 24:32–34).

Take careful note of the location from which Jesus spoke these words. He was standing at Jerusalem's Temple Mount, which I call "ground zero" for Bible prophecy. As the disciples asked questions about when the end would come, Jesus responded. It was then that He told them all these prophetic events would happen in a single generation. I want you to know that many of these events have already taken place in *our* generation with more sure to follow. We are *that* generation.

On the Day of Pentecost, the Holy Spirit fell upon the Church. The apostle Peter stood to speak. He opened with his explanation of the unusual events that were taking place by saying, "But this is what was spoken by the prophet Joel" (Acts 2:16). Peter went on to tell the people how Joel's prophecies were being fulfilled before their eyes—*this is what was spoken.* I am telling you right now as you read this book—*this is what was spoken.* In this generation, God is fulfilling what He promised long ago.

Later in this book I will explain in greater detail why I believe Israel is God's super-sign announcing the arrival of the end times. For now, though, I will give you *five specific examples* of the way God has woven the prophecies about Israel in the Bible into a beautiful pattern.

1. Israel Is Regathered Twice.

The Bible prophesies that the people of Israel will be gathered together again twice after being scattered. The prophet Isaiah wrote:

> "And in that day there shall be a Root of Jesse,
> Who shall stand as a banner to the people;

For the Gentiles shall seek Him,

And His resting place shall be glorious."

It shall come to pass in that day

That the Lord shall set His hand again the second time

To recover the remnant of His people who are left,

From Assyria and Egypt,

From Pathros and Cush,

From Elam and Shinar,

From Hamath and the islands of the sea.

He will set up a banner for the nations,

And will assemble the outcasts of Israel,

And gather together the dispersed of Judah

From the four corners of the earth (Isaiah 11:10–12).

For 70 years, a defeated Israel would both suffer and languish in Babylon as a result of their idolatry and rejection of God. But He would not allow them to stay there forever. God promised to bring them back to their land, which is exactly what He did. In 586 BC the return began, and by 516 BC the Temple in Jerusalem was rebuilt. Then God fulfilled His promise again in 1948. For almost two millennia, the Hebrew people had been scattered around the world. They had shown a remarkable ability to both survive and thrive through various times of comfort and persecution. The extreme persecution under the Nazis precipitated a final and miraculous move back to their homeland for the second time—just as Isaiah foretold.

GOD'S MESSAGES ABOUT
THE FUTURE ARE OUR ONLY
RELIABLE SOURCE OF
TRUTH ABOUT IT.

2. Israel Is Born in One Day.

Isaiah wrote again:

Who has heard such a thing?
Who has seen such things?
Shall the earth be made to give birth in one day?
Or shall a nation be born at once?
For as soon as Zion was in labor,
She gave birth to her children (Isaiah 66:8).

On May 14, 1948, Great Britain's colonial mandate for Palestine expired, and they released the territory. Before the day was over, David Ben-Gurion, the head of the Jewish Agency, announced the establishment of the State of Israel. US President Harry Truman was quick to recognize the new nation on the very same day. Other nations were slower to follow Truman's lead, but that is the birthdate of the State of Israel as a recognized government. It happened on a single day—May 14, 1948.

3. Israel Is Regathered from the North.

As the nation began to build, from where would the people come? Many Jews lived in Europe or the Americas, and they came by the thousands. Large groups of people came from Russia. Between January 1989 and December 2002, 1.1 million Russian Jews immigrated to Israel. Russian President Mikhail Gorbachev opened the borders, allowing Jews to leave and unwittingly fulfilling Jeremiah's prophecy, penned 2,500 years before:

"Therefore behold, the days are coming," says the LORD, "that it shall no more be said, 'The LORD lives who brought up the children of Israel from the land of Egypt,' but, 'The LORD lives who brought up the children of Israel from the land of the north and from all the lands where He had driven them.' For I will bring them back into their land which I gave to their fathers" (Jeremiah 16:14–15).

One amazing result of the Russian Jewish influx into Palestine is that many of these new immigrants were Messianic Jews who formed new congregations, something that would have been unheard of not very many years ago.

4. Jerusalem Is Re-taken by the Jews.

After many years of desolation and control by Gentile (non-Jewish) nations, Jesus said Israel would be re-captured by the Jewish People. He said in Luke's gospel:

> But when you see Jerusalem surrounded by armies, then know that its desolation is near. Then let those who are in Judea flee to the mountains, let those who are in the midst of her depart, and let not those who are in the country enter her. For these are the days of vengeance, that all things which are written may be fulfilled. But woe to those who are pregnant and to those who are nursing babies in those days! For there will be great distress in the land and wrath upon this people. And they will fall by the edge of the sword, and be led away captive into all nations. And Jerusalem will be trampled by Gentiles until the times of the Gentiles are fulfilled (Luke 21:20–24).

The beginning of the fulfillment of this prophecy was in AD 70. The Roman general Titus had invaded Israel, finally destroying the city of Jerusalem. The Jewish people were scattered throughout the world (the Diaspora), where they would remain for approximately 1,900 years. In 1948 they began to return to their homeland. Then in 1967 Israel engaged in the Arab-Israeli Six Day War. On June 10, 1967, the Jews regained control of the city, and it remains in their hands today. For me, this is the most significant prophetic event of my lifetime.

5. The Land of Israel Is Divided, Coupled with Worldwide Anti-Semitism.

Under pressure from the United Nations, Israel has been forced to relinquish control of portions of the West Bank, the Gaza Strip, and the Sinai Peninsula. They have been under increasing international pressure, including from the US, to concede East Jerusalem to the Palestinians. In subsequent chapters I will discuss the ongoing opposition to Israel and the nation's efforts to defend itself. These events were foretold by the prophet Joel:

> For behold, in those days and at that time,
> When I bring back the captives of Judah and Jerusalem,
> I will also gather all nations,
> And bring them down to the Valley of Jehoshaphat;
> And I will enter into judgment with them there
> On account of My people, My heritage Israel,

Whom they have scattered among the nations;
They have also divided up My land (Joel 3:1–2).

GOD'S UNBROKEN PATTERN

You may have heard the old saying, "The Bible is more up-to-date than tomorrow's newspaper." I want to assure you that saying is not mere "preacher talk." God's biblical prophecies are clear and verifiable—they are undeniably true, and the pieces fall together into a remarkable, unbroken pattern. God said that in the same period He would regather Israel from the nations of the world, He would also enter into judgment with the world. What does this mean? We are seeing the Bible's prophecies fulfilled in front of our eyes. In the next section I will tell you about some of the other prophecies of the Bible that are not yet fulfilled, but some of them are in the process of coming to fruition even as I am writing this book. Jesus is coming for His Church very soon. Don't wait to prepare your heart to meet Him or to witness to those who do not yet know Him. The time is now!

---•---

JESUS IS COMING FOR HIS CHURCH VERY SOON.

2

THE MIRACLE OF ISRAEL

When World War II ended, accounts of the Nazi atrocities upon the Jewish people of Europe first began trickling in and then became a deluge. Germany bore undeniable guilt, but it soon became clear that almost every free nation had committed sins of both commission and omission against the Jewish people. Some countries had simply ignored their plight; others took roles that were more active in the slaughter. Enough Jewish blood had been spilled to dirty the hands of nearly every nation in the world. Active killing of Jewish people stopped with the surrender of the Third Reich, but most surviving Jews no longer had homes to which they could return. Even if they could go back, many didn't want to return. A new predicament replaced the Nazi onslaught: what could be done with all the displaced surviving Jews?

Almost 2,000 miles from western Europe, another crisis had been brewing for several decades. In 1917 the British government issued the Balfour Declaration, a public statement announcing support for the establishment of "a national home for the Jewish people" in Palestine.[2] At the time, the region was controlled by the Ottoman Empire, a Muslim majority caliphate governing much of the Middle East. By the end of World War I, only a small Jewish population lived in Palestine.

Although the United States supported the Balfour Declaration in principle, US President Franklin D. Roosevelt had assured Palestinian Arabs in 1945 that the US would not intervene without first consulting both Arabs and Jews.[3] And while Britain still held a colonial mandate for Palestine, it was set to expire in May 1948.[4] The official British position had been modified significantly since 1917 to oppose a Jewish state alongside the Arab state in Palestine. The British also did not support a large immigration of displaced Jews into the region. Great Britain wanted to maintain good relations with the Arabs for economic and political reasons. For the most part, two of the three significant members of World War II's Allied Forces either opposed a Jewish state or were indifferent to it. The future for a Jewish state in Palestine didn't look hopeful.

On April 12, 1945, President Roosevelt died of a hemorrhagic stroke at his Little White House home in Warm Springs, Georgia. Under the leadership of new President Harry S. Truman, the Allied forces prevailed on September 2, 1945. Soon after taking office, Truman appointed a group of Middle East experts to explore the options for the Palestinian region, including the possibility of a Jewish state in the region. The Americans entered into negotiations with the British to discuss the issue.

In May 1946, Truman approved a proposal to admit 100,000 displaced Jews into Palestine, and in October he declared his support for the creation of a Jewish state. By 1947 the United Nations Special Commission on Palestine recommended the partition of Palestine into both an Arab and a Jewish state. In November 1947, the UN adopted a resolution that would divide Palestine when the British were scheduled to give up their colonial mandate the following May.[5] As the date drew near, the US leadership grew increasingly concerned about the possibility of an all-out war because Arab states had already threatened an attack.

Despite the Arab concern, President Truman decided to recognize a new state of Israel. On May 14, 1948, the British fulfilled their obligation to release Palestine. By the end of the day, David Ben-Gurion, the head of the Jewish Agency, announced the establishment of the State of Israel. While many nations were slow to recognize the new Jewish nation, the US, under the leadership of President Truman, recognized the new nation on the same day.[6]

The history of the birth of modern-day Israel is more detailed than I have laid out here, although this may be more information than you wanted to know. However, I want you to recognize it was not an easy process. In fact, the formation of the nation of Israel was highly unlikely, if not impossible. None of it was a coincidence, though. It was all prophesied in Scripture thousands of years ago and is more proof of the authority of the

Bible and end times prophecy. I believe without a doubt that God Himself orchestrated all these events.

I want to share with you how I fell in love with Israel, because it is supernatural and could have never happened without God's intervention. One day my wife and I were casually browsing around a Christian bookstore, and I saw a poster on the wall. It bore one simple word, "Israel," and had a picture of a menorah (a Jewish lampstand). I had never focused on the word "Israel" before and certainly didn't understand the significance of the Jewish people. Despite my lack of knowledge, though, I supernaturally fell deeply in love with Israel and the Jewish people the very instant my eyes fell on that poster. It was as if I had just seen the most beautiful woman in the world and immediately fell in love with her.

After staring at that poster for a few minutes, I approached the bookstore owner at the front counter and asked him, "What does that poster over there mean?" He proceeded to tell me about the nation of Israel and the Jewish people from the Bible's perspective. But what meant the most to me was when he told me that Jesus was, and is, Jewish. That event was so meaningful, and my love for Israel has only grown through the years.

Some of my readers, like me, are likely too young to have been alive when Israel became a nation, but we are still in that generation of the birth of Israel's nationhood. Israel's existence is a pure miracle; God masterfully orchestrated the nations and powers of the world for it to become a reality. For the end to come, the nation of Israel must exist. For almost 2,000 years the Jewish people were scattered all over the world, but their nation was reborn as a physical and geographical reality on one day in May of 1948. God is gathering them again to their homeland as an answer to Bible prophecy.

THE BIBLE AND ISRAEL

The Bible contains the story of God and His love for people. More specifically, it is about His covenant with a particular people—the nation of Israel. I am reminded of an epigram once penned as a short anti-Semitic ditty by British Journalist William Norman Ewer:

How odd
of God
To choose
the Jews.

Numerous authors and politicians countered this dismissive insult with their own clever poems. The following response has been attributed both to Cecil Brown and to Ogden Nash:

But not so odd
As those who choose
A Jewish God
Yet spurn the Jews.

Although Ewer intended it as a slur, the question remains, *Why has God chosen Israel?* Professor Jon Huntzinger of The King's University gives this helpful explanation:

> By showing His willingness to give salvation and victory to the Israelites, who are smaller and weaker than their foes, God gives us reason to believe He will do the same for anyone else.[7]

Through Israel, God would show His love and bring salvation to the entire human race. In His great plan for the world, Israel is not inconsequential; it is essential, and the Bible demonstrates this fact on every page. Consider some of the great truths about Israel the Scriptures show us:

1. They Were Created by God

This is how Israel began:

> Now the LORD had said to Abram:
> "Get out of your country,
> From your family
> And from your father's house,
> To a land that I will show you.
> I will make you a great nation;
> I will bless you
> And make your name great;
> And you shall be a blessing.
> I will bless those who bless you,
> And I will curse him who curses you;
> And in you all the families of the earth shall be blessed"
> (Genesis 12:1–3).

THROUGH ISRAEL, GOD WOULD
SHOW HIS LOVE AND BRING
SALVATION TO THE ENTIRE
HUMAN RACE.

The Bible repeatedly affirms that Israel is the only nation ever created by God. There has never been another nation formed by God Himself. In fact, Israel's existence is a testimony to God's existence. The survival of the people of Israel is one proof of God's active providence in the lives of His people.

2. They Are in an Eternal Covenant with God

God also made this covenant with Abraham and his descendants:

> "I *am* Almighty God; walk before Me and be blameless. And I will make My covenant between Me and you, and will multiply you exceedingly." Then Abram fell on his face, and God talked with him, saying: "As for Me, behold, My covenant is with you, and you shall be a father of many nations. No longer shall your name be called Abram, but your name shall be Abraham; for I have made you a father of many nations. I will make you exceedingly fruitful; and I will make nations of you, and kings shall come from you. And I will establish My covenant between Me and you and your descendants after you in their generations, for an everlasting covenant, to be God to you and your descendants after you. Also I give to you and your descendants after you the land in which you are a stranger, all the land of Canaan, as an everlasting possession; and I will be their God" (Genesis 17:1–8).

Yes, God made a covenant with His people Israel, and it is everlasting. This means it is still in force to this present day. Someone might wonder, *When God uses the word* Israel, *what does He mean? Is it the land or the people?* The answer is both belong to God. His everlasting covenant is a land promise *and* a people promise.

Salvation comes only through the blood sacrifice of Jesus Christ. A Jewish person cannot be eternally saved without receiving Jesus by faith. Nevertheless, God maintains a special covenant with His people Israel. That doesn't mean that God loves Jews and doesn't love Arabs or non-Jewish people. God loves all people of all races, and Jesus died on the cross for everyone.

But Jews are special to God by covenant. We should all remember that God made a promise to Abraham related to the Jews that is still in force today. God said to Abraham:

> I will bless those who bless you,
> And I will curse him who curses you (Genesis 12:3).

To demonstrate the reality of that promise, there has never been a world power that persecuted the Jews that remained great. It is also true of individuals, groups, religions, and all nations.

3. A Blessing to the Nations

God said to Abraham, "In you all the families of the earth shall be blessed" (Genesis 12:3). God not only promised blessing, but He also promised that His people Israel would bless others. And God's promise has been fulfilled many times over as the Jewish people have blessed the world more than any other nation. How can I make this claim? Consider just three of the gifts the Jewish people have given the world.

- First, the Jewish people gave us the *most important man* in all human history: our Lord and Savior Jesus of Nazareth. He is our Messiah, and He is a Jew. How, then, could any of His followers be anti-Semitic? (Someone who is anti-Semitic is against the Jews or hates Jewish people.) I will never understand how a *Christian* could also be an *anti-Semite.* It's a contradiction in terms. Note that I didn't say Jesus *was* a Jew; I said He *is* a Jew. Our Savior is Jewish—for all eternity.

- Second, the Jewish people gave us the gift of the *most important book* in the history of the world: the Bible. In fact, Jewish people wrote every word in it. This 100 percent Jewish book has given us the light by which we can live our lives and know God's intention for us even after we leave the world.

- Finally, the Jewish people gave us *the most important organization:* the Church. On the Day of Pentecost, when the Holy Spirit descended and the Church was born, 100 percent of those who first received the Spirit were Jewish. One hundred percent of the people in the audience at the first Christian sermon were Jewish. By grace (theirs and God's), we who are non-Jews (Gentiles) were invited into the Church. Those early Jewish believers listened to the Holy Spirit, and as a result we were allowed into the Church.

The most important man. The most important book. The most important organization. Those are just three of the gifts the Jewish people have given to us. We bless the Jews, for by them God has blessed all the families of the world.

ISRAEL IS GOD'S BELLWETHER

The leading sheep in a flock is called a *bellwether*. It wears a bell around its neck and is first in line of all the other sheep. Metaphorically, a bellwether is an indicator or predictor of an event that will happen sometime in the future. Israel is God's bellwether. In a real sense Israel is God's prophetic super-sign and stopwatch. This is what the prophet Joel says concerning the end times:

> The sun shall be turned into darkness,
> And the moon into blood,
> Before the coming of the great and awesome day of the LORD.
> [That's the end; that's the final Day of Judgment.]
> And it shall come to pass
> *That* whoever calls on the name of the LORD
> Shall be saved.
> For in Mount Zion and in Jerusalem there shall be deliverance,
> As the LORD has said,
> Among the remnant whom the LORD calls.

For behold, in those days and at that time,

When I bring back the captives of Judah and Jerusalem,

 I will also gather all nations,

And bring them down to the Valley of Jehoshaphat;

And I will enter into judgment with them there

On account of My people, My heritage Israel,

Whom they have scattered among the nations;

They have also divided up My land (Joel 2:31–3:2).

This return began in 1948 and has been happening ever since. God says He will bring them to the Valley of *Jehoshaphat,* which means '*Yahweh* has judged.' This prophecy is referring to Armageddon, where the final scene of human history will occur as all the nations of the world march against Israel to destroy it. Joel delivers an end time prophecy, which is more up to date than our morning news. In fact, it is unfolding before us every single day and is more proof that we are the final generation.

I will point to another common metaphor: the canary in the coal mine. Today coal miners have access to sophisticated scientific instruments and gauges that determine the air quality in mines. However, coal miners used to rely on caged birds (canaries in particular) to measure whether a particular mine was safe for human workers. The respiratory and nervous systems of canaries are much more sensitive than those of humans. Therefore, if a canary became physically distressed, usually because of carbon monoxide levels, then it was time for humans to vacate the mine. Israel is the proverbial canary in the coal mine for all humanity. What happens to Israel is God's super-sign of what will soon happen to the entire world. *Four contemporary events* demonstrate this fact. These happenings also fulfill the passage from the prophecy in Joel 2.

1. Rebirth and Re-gathering

Joel's prophecy predicts the rebirth of Israel and the re-gathering of the Jewish people. God says, "In that day and at that time, when I gather my people from the nations." In God's plan the end times began in earnest on May 14, 1948, and we can know that is true because in Joel chapter three God is speaking in the first person and is effectively saying, "When I bring back My people from all the nations, the Battle of Armageddon is going to happen in the same timeframe. When I bring back my people into their land, in that same period of time, I'm going to enter into judgment with all the nations of the world because of how they have treated My people and how they have divided up My land."

2. Division of Land

Joel foretells the division of the land of Israel. Consider that from 2006 to 2016, the United Nations Human Rights Council criticized Israel 68 times—three times more than any other nation. And of the 97 resolutions adopted by the United Nations General Assembly between 2012 and 2015, 83 were against Israel.[8] The UN has called Israel a "racist state," and some UN members have even accused her of apartheid.[9] Think about the irony of that accusation considering the horrors Jewish people have experienced over the last century.

Clearly, the UN opposes the nation of Israel, but this also fulfills an end time prophecy. The UN, including the US, has compelled Israel to concede land several times in a ploy called "Land for Peace."[10] Israel continues to yield land, yet there is no lasting peace. Each concession of land to the Palestinians simply leads to renewed aggression from them. Usually it places hostile Palestinians in closer proximity to Israeli cities. When the Palestinians gain land, it means more opportunities for terrorist acts and increased accuracy for lethal missiles.

In 2005, under the leadership of President Bush, the United States compelled Israel to leave most of the Gaza Strip—Israeli land—and turn it over to the Palestinians. Seven days later, Hurricane Katrina struck the US Gulf Coast. Rabbi Ovadia Yosef openly declared that natural disaster to be "God's retribution for America's actions."[11]

What God says in Joel's prophecy is happening in the current day. The UN and some political leaders in the US are actively working to force Israel into a two-state solution with the Palestinians. This initiative is an attempt to compel Israel to recognize a Palestinian state.[12] However, this plan has two apparent drawbacks. First, the Palestinians have actively terrorized Israelis and are led by admitted terrorists. Second, the Palestinians leaders have no intention to recognize Israel's right to exist. In fact, they have an avowed pledge to Israel's ultimate and immediate destruction.[13] Why would you recognize someone who refuses to recognize you and wants to annihilate you? Why have some leaders in the US been trying to force the Israelis to concede their land to terrorists? Let me be clear: I am not claiming all Palestinians are terrorists, but I am saying their leaders have a long history of terroristic acts.

God declares, "I'm going to bring back My people. From all over the world, I'm going to re-gather them. And I'm going to enter into judgment with the people who are dividing up My land." I am telling you, on biblical grounds, that the land belongs to God, and the land belongs to Israel. The Jewish people have only a tiny piece of land in the Middle East, yet they can't even rest there because the nations and multinational organizations of the world keep trying to force them to give it up. These prophecies, many of which were written well over 2,000 years ago, say the final scene of human history will be set with the entire world converging in battle against a tiny, insignificant nation in the Middle East. This offensive is unfolding before our eyes.

3. Coming Armageddon

Zechariah delivered this important prophecy from the Lord:

Behold, I will make Jerusalem a cup of drunkenness to all the surrounding peoples, when they lay siege against Judah and Jerusalem.
And it shall happen in that day that I will make Jerusalem a very
heavy stone for all peoples; all who would heave it away will surely
be cut in pieces, though all nations of the earth are gathered against
it (Zechariah 12:2–3).

What does it mean when the Lord says Jerusalem will be "a
very heavy stone?" Israel will find herself in an impossible political situation.

On December 6, 2017, President Donald Trump announced
that the United States would begin recognizing Jerusalem rather
than Tel Aviv as Israel's capital and move the US Embassy to
Jerusalem.[14] Global leaders and even some Americans became
apoplectic. International condemnation for the US decision was
quick and almost unanimous. The UN Security Council held an
emergency meeting the next day, and 14 of 15 members condemned the US decision. The United States was the only member to vote against the motion, constituting a veto vote. None
of the US allies stood behind the decision.[15] Only seven nations
(Guatemala, Honduras, Marshall Islands, Micronesia, Nauru,
Palau, and Togo) stood with the US and Israel on the matter.[16]
None of them are members of the Security Council, though. All
members of the European Union reaffirmed their commitment
to a Palestinian State with its capital in East Jerusalem.

Palestinian officials were even more vocal in their disapproval, saying the decision disqualified the US from partici-

pation. Leaders of Hamas called for a new military offensive against the Israelis. Following President Trump's announcement, Palestinians angrily and violently demonstrated in the West Bank and Gaza Strip, as well as in several other countries.[17] Still, on May 14, 2018, the US embassy officially opened in Jerusalem.[18] It was the 70th anniversary of Israel becoming a nation. Before the day ended, deadly violence had broken out on the Gaza border.[19]

Until this point in history, even the US had opposed the move of Israel's national capital to Jerusalem. Jerusalem has become "a very heavy stone," in direct fulfillment of Zechariah's prophecy. The fight for Jerusalem isn't over, even if there is a brief, uneasy pause in the battle.

4. Blood Moons

God created the sun, moon, and stars as signals in the sky to establish His time clock for the feasts of Israel and as signs of significant events. In a subsequent chapter I will discuss some of the most significant signs in the sky, but I want to tell you about one such sign now because it relates specifically to what God is doing in Israel.

The prophet Joel wrote the following:

The sun shall be turned into darkness,
And the moon into blood,
Before the coming of the great and awesome day of the LORD
(Joel 2:31; see also Acts 2:20).

A blood moon is the same as a lunar eclipse when the moon turns red. Four consecutive blood moons are called a tetrad. Before 1949 the convergence of four consecutive blood moons on Jewish holy days hadn't occurred for 500 years, and it will not happen again for another 500 years.[20] Over a very short time, God has been hanging an advertisement in the heavens and saying to us, "Look! I'm doing something very special here." Again, the Bible told us this would happen.

The first time there were four blood moons on Jewish holy days in successive years was in 1492 and 1493. Most of us in the Americas remember 1492 as the year when "Columbus sailed the ocean blue" and came to the Americas. But did you know that in 1492 King Ferdinand and Queen Isabella expelled the Jews from Spain if they would not convert to Catholicism? Did you also know that many historians believe Christopher Columbus was secretly a Jew and the true purpose of his voyage to America was to find a safe place for the Jews to live?

The second time there were four blood moons on Jewish holy days in successive years was in 1949 and 1950. Israel became a nation in one day on May 14, 1948 but was not established as a government until 1949. The third time it happened was in 1967 and 1968. The Jews took full control of the city of Jerusalem in 1967 after the Six Day War. The fourth and last time it happened was in 2014 and 2015. And in those years we also saw a total and a partial solar eclipse on Jewish holy days.

Undoubtedly, God is sending signals in the sky related to the end of the age and the return of Jesus just as the book of Joel and Jesus Himself said He would. And these are very important signals. Here is what I believe the significance of each of the tetrad of blood moons has meant since 1492:

- *The beginning of the re-gathering of God's holy people (1492 and 1493).*

    After the Roman General Titus defeated the Jewish people in AD 70, many were taken captive and then scattered around the world. From that time on, they had no place to call home. The events of 1492 were the beginning of a re-gathering of the Jewish people by God.

- *The re-establishment of God's holy nation (1949 and 1950).*

    The tetrad of blood moons during this time was a shout of rejoicing in heaven that the Jewish homeland was officially reborn and the Jewish people could return from all around the world. This event was the fulfillment of many Old and New Testament prophecies, and according to Joel chapter three, it was the beginning of the countdown of the final generation.

- *The re-unification of God's Holy City (1967 and 1968).*

    When the nation of Israel was reborn in 1948, the Jews controlled only half of the city of Jerusalem. Then in

1967 Israel regained all of Jerusalem as her capital in the Six Day War or the Third Arab-Israeli War.[21] *I consider this the single most important event related to the end times that has happened during my lifetime.* Four blood moons occurred on Jewish holy days over the next 24 months.[22] In Luke 21:24 Jesus prophesied the defeat of Israel, the destruction of Jerusalem, the scattering of the Jews around the world, and that Jerusalem would be trodden under foot by the Gentiles (non-Jews) until the times of the Gentiles were fulfilled. That occurred in 1967 and was a major prophetic fulfillment signaling the soon return of Jesus.

- *The Jews prepare to rebuild God's holy Temple (2014 and 2015).*

After the tumultuous Gaza Conflict, four blood moons happened again during Jewish feasts.[23] Although the Jewish people have wanted to rebuild the Temple since the re-establishment of Israel in 1948, the movement has been largely squelched, mostly by international interference. Despite opposition, the calls to rebuild have been growing significantly as The Temple Institute and other Jewish religious groups have been diligently preparing to rebuild the Temple and reinstitute all ceremonies, sacrifices, and worship according to biblical patterns and practices. On August 28, 2018, a red heifer was born in Israel, and this animal currently qualifies as "unblemished." This incident is critical because a third Temple cannot be built until a red heifer exists that can qualify as a sacrifice and its ashes used for cleansing and preparing the Temple, according to Numbers chapter 19. According to Jewish tradition there have only been nine red heifers sacrificed since Moses, and the tenth will herald the Messianic Age. This new red heifer would qualify as the tenth. I believe the blood moons of 2014 and 2015 announced the season of rebuilding the Temple and the soon return of Jesus. It is also my opinion that believers will not see the Temple rebuilt because the Rapture will occur first. Then the Antichrist will confirm a seven-year covenant with Israel (Daniel 9:27). I believe this covenant with the Antichrist will allow the Jews to rebuild their Temple in exchange for them conceding part of the Temple Mount to the Muslims and East Jerusalem as the capital for the Palestinians. I believe this event is a fulfillment of this prophecy:

I was given a reed like a measuring rod. And the angel stood, saying, "Rise and measure the temple of God, the altar, and those who worship there. But leave out the court which is outside the temple, and do not measure it, for it has been given to the Gentiles. And they will tread the holy city underfoot for forty-two months" (Revelation 11:1–2).

This prophecy relates to the first three and a half years of the Tribulation when the Jews will be allowed to rebuild their Temple but not given the entire Temple Mount. The apostle John also prophesies that the Holy City will be trampled underfoot by Gentiles for 42 months, which is three and a half years.

I am thankful that our God speaks to us in unmistakable ways so we can be properly prepared. When Jesus returns and the end comes, no person on the planet will have an excuse for not being ready. Not only did God tell us through His Word, but He has also been shouting it in the skies. In a later chapter, I will discuss other prophetic signs in the heavens related to the end times, but the blood moons relate specifically to the fulfillment of Joel's prophecy about the nation of Israel.

5. Global Hatred

In Joel 3 the Lord tells the nations of the world that He will bring them into judgment for how they have treated His people Israel. Anti-Semitism has not disappeared. In fact, it is rising in America and Europe. Many Jews are forced to leave Europe and return to Israel or come to the US for fear of their safety. Anti-Semitism is brewing all over the world, but the Bible says this will happen at the very end of time. God declares,

> For behold, in those days and at that time,
> When I bring back the captives of Judah and Jerusalem,
> I will also gather all nations,
> And bring them down to the Valley of Jehoshaphat;

And I will enter into judgment with them there
On account of My people, My heritage Israel,
Whom they have scattered among the nations;
They have also divided up My land (Joel 3:1–2).

In AD 70, the Roman general Titus (later an emperor) defeated the Jewish people in Israel, and survivors were scattered around the world. [24] Jesus prophesied in Luke 21:24: "They will fall by the edge of the sword, and be led away captive into all nations. And Jerusalem will be trampled by Gentiles until the times of the Gentiles are fulfilled." Then in 1967 Jerusalem came under the control of the nation of Israel. This marked the end of the age of the Gentiles.

A MESSAGE FOR THIS GENERATION

In a single generation we will see all end times events fulfilled. Jesus said, "Assuredly, I say to you, this generation will by no means pass away till all these things take place" (Matthew 24:34). He was speaking about the times we are living in. He wasn't talking about His generation while He was here on earth. All those people died.

You might wonder, *But Jimmy, hasn't every generation had signs of the end times?* Yes, they have. Each generation has had earthquakes and famines. Every generation has seen some crazy leaders who people thought could be the Antichrist. So, you're exactly right. Even so, the final generation won't have *some* signs; it will have *every* sign.

The Bible proclaims the end will happen within one generation. But how long is a generation? In Psalm 90, Moses wrote:

> The days of our lives *are* seventy years;
> And if by reason of strength *they are* eighty years (v. 10).

On May 14, 2018, the State of Israel turned 70 years old. Five months earlier, on December 6, 2017, US President Donald Trump recognized Jerusalem as Israel's true and legitimate national capital and began plans to move the US embassy from Tel Aviv to Jerusalem. For the first time since King Cyrus, who ruled approximately 2,500 years ago, a major world leader has formally recognized Jerusalem as Israel's capital city. Yes, I believe the clock is moving forward very rapidly. If the generation Jesus was referring to is 70 years, then we are already past it. If it is 80 years, we aren't that far away. Either way, these are fascinating days.

I will say again that I have neither the right nor the ability to set the exact dates when the end will come, but I'm telling you what the Bible says. Jesus said the generation that sees the *beginning* of the end will see all things fulfilled. The end times are upon us, even now. They are a compressed amount of time in God's mind, and what we see happening in Israel today is proof.

WHEN JESUS RETURNS AND
THE END COMES, NO PERSON
ON THE PLANET WILL HAVE AN
EXCUSE FOR NOT BEING READY.

3

ISRAEL—GOD'S
SUPER-SIGN

In the previous chapter I discussed the signs of the end times as they relate to Israel and the city of Jerusalem. Yes, Israel is at a tipping point, and the Bible tells us what will soon happen. The nation of Israel will face two major wars before the end. One of those wars is recorded in Psalm 83, and it seems the beginnings of that war might have already started.

THE GOG AND MAGOG WAR

However, a second and larger war is also coming, which the Bible says will involve Gog and Magog. Ezekiel delivered a prophecy about this coming war:

> Now the word of the LORD came to me, saying, "Son of man, set your face against Gog, of the land of Magog, the prince of Rosh, Meshech, and Tubal, and prophesy against him, and say, 'Thus says the Lord GOD: "Behold, I *am* against you, O Gog, the prince of Rosh, Meshech, and Tubal. I will turn you around, put hooks into your jaws, and lead you out, with all your army, horses, and horse-

men, all splendidly clothed, a great company *with* bucklers and shields, all of them handling swords. Persia, Ethiopia, and Libya are with them, all of them *with* shield and helmet; Gomer and all its troops; the house of Togarmah *from* the far north and all its troops—many people *are* with you.

Prepare yourself and be ready, you and all your companies that are gathered about you; and be a guard for them. After many days you will be visited. In the latter years you will come into the land of those brought back from the sword *and* gathered from many people on the mountains of Israel, which had long been desolate; they were brought out of the nations, and now all of them dwell safely. You will ascend, coming like a storm, covering the land like a cloud, you and all your troops and many peoples with you"'" (Ezekiel 38:1–9).

The war Ezekiel foretells has not happened yet, but it is coming soon. In fact, the events leading up to it are happening even as I write these words.

What nations was Ezekiel prophesying about? Here is part of the list:

- Gog and Magog are believed by many to be Russia.

- Persia is Iran (Iranians are not Arabs; they are Persians).

- This prophecy includes parts of modern-day Iraq and Afghanistan.

- Ethiopia includes parts of modern-day Sudan and southern Egypt.

- Togarmah is Turkey.

Ezekiel also includes other nations, but the ones I just mentioned are the primary players. When Ezekiel recorded this prophecy, the religion of Islam did not yet exist. It was not formed until the seventh century, so the prophet would not have known he was describing the contemporary Muslim world, which covers many countries and includes those who have radicalized against the Jews and the nation of Israel.

Today Russia is aiding Iran in its construction of nuclear facilities.[25] The Iranian government claims to need these facilities to expand the nation's energy options,[26] but something more sinister is afoot. Keep in mind that Iran is not the entire name of the country; it is the Islamic Republic of Iran and has a stated purpose to destroy the nation of Israel. Radical Islamists, which include the Iranians and ISIS, believe Allah has called them to destroy Israel and usher in the end of the age with their own version of the messiah.[27]

Simple politicians do not govern the Iranians. Instead, their religious leaders, called Mullahs, control the political machine and the direction of the nation. If you want to understand the government of Iran, then just imagine a select group of pastors having the final authority over the President of the United States, Congress, and the Supreme Court. That is what is happening in Iran. These leaders are extremist Muslims, which explains Iran's current situation. I should say that I don't believe the majority of the Iranian citizens hold these extreme beliefs. In fact, I believe overall they are kind and intelligent people who love the US and respect Jewish people. However, they are not the ones we most often see on the news when their government denounces Israel and calls America "The Great Satan."[28] That sentiment comes from the Muslim-controlled government that wants to destroy Israel and anyone who supports her.

Because of this stated objective to decimate Israel, Iran should never be allowed to obtain serious weaponry, which could create massive destruction in Israel or any other nation. Western nations, including the US, should never allow the Iranians to develop nuclear technology or nuclear weaponry. If you hear that leaders in the US have taken a hardline stance against Iran, it is because they know the stated goals and behind-the-scenes maneuverings of that government.

In the late 1970s, Sadaam Hussein, Iraq's supreme leader, oversaw the construction of a nuclear plant southeast of Baghdad. He claimed he wanted to expand his nation's energy options, but part of his agenda also included the ultimate destruction of Israel. On June 7, 1981, Israeli bombers daringly conducted Operation Babylon (also known as Operation Opera), which targeted Iraq's nuclear reactor.[29] Israel rightfully declared the operation an act of self-defense. Most international experts agreed that the Iraqis were less than one month from reaching a critical point in creating a nuclear weapon. While some international observers denounced Israel's actions at the time, it is clear in hindsight that the Israelis took necessary and decisive actions to ensure their own survival.

As I write these words, tensions between Iran and Israel have not subsided. Iran is engaging in a proxy war with the Israelis in Syria.[30] During US President Barak Obama's administration, Israel considered bombing Iran. Some reports claim the US government threatened to shoot down Israeli planes if they attempted an attack.[31] Whether or not these reports are true, the opposition was real. Israel stood alone, isolated in the Middle East. Under the Trump administration, US relations with Israel have improved, but tensions with Iran continue to grow.

Iranian President Hassan Rouhani has said he may withdraw his country from an agreement to limit Iran's ability to develop nuclear weapons. In June 2019, he announced that Iran would restart its uranium enrichment program.[32] If so, the Iranians will be able to develop a nuclear weapon within a year or less. Rouhani's claims that Iran will use the uranium for civilian electrical power grids have been met with skepticism from the US and its allies. On June 17, 2019, Israeli Prime Minister Benjamin Netanyahu said, "Israel will not allow Iran to obtain nuclear weapons."[33] Historically, Israel has been unafraid to take preventive measures to protect itself, including launching preemptive strikes on nations it perceives as threatening, such as it did in Iraq. As the situation becomes more volatile, unilateral Israeli action becomes more justifiable and probable. Also likely is international disapproval of Israel's necessary actions to ensure survival.

Israel's long-held counterproliferation policy is known as the Begin Doctrine, which permits Israeli forces to wage preventive strikes against any hostile nation that engages in weapons programs directly threatening Israel's security.[34] Israel has acted on this doctrine as the nation sees fit. For decades the Israeli military has destroyed chemical, nuclear, and computer technology facilities and capabilities across the Middle East. The current Israeli government maintains a strong position that it has the option to strike Iran in self-defense. Netanyahu has warned, "Iranian acquisition of nuclear weapons would be infinitely more costly than any scenario you can imagine to stop it."[35] If Iran does restart uranium enrichment, then strikes might become inevitable.

Until recently, ISIS controlled half of Syria and had outposts throughout the region. The US waged a defensive war against the rogue state, which had an aggressive program to control the nations around Israel and ultimately bring about Israel's destruction. Remarkably, the Bible describes this situation more than 2,500 years ago. The picture Ezekiel draws in his prophecy is the exact current geopolitical reality. Those nations still exist in a modern form, are still in union with each other, and still hate Israel.

You may wonder, *How will this great war begin?* I will state the answer from my own opinion, but it is not an unstudied opinion. The nation of Israel must defend herself. She simply cannot allow Iran to perfect its nuclear technology, which will lead to nuclear weaponry. It is a clear and present existential threat to the nation. I believe Israel will ultimately have to strike Iran first and with decisive force. The Iranians have a powerful military, but Israel is more powerful than all other Middle Eastern countries combined. The Israelis possess highly-sophisticated weapons and technology. Even more, the people of Israel are full of courage and resolve. They will use all necessary means to preserve their nation.

The Russian government has warned Israel that this "possible military scenario against Iran will be catastrophic for the region" and that they "should consider the consequences of such action for themselves."[36] Through Ezekiel, God says, "I'm going to put a hook in your jaw, and I'm going to drag you down to the mountains of Israel" (Ezekiel 38:4; 39:2). In fact, Ezekiel continues by saying that when all these nations invade them, the people of Israel will not have to fire a single shot. God says to Israel's enemies, "I'm going to kill you Myself." I believe this is God's response to Islamic Jihad. It will take seven months to bury the dead and another seven years to clear the debris, according to Ezekiel chapter 39. That's how catastrophic God says it will be.

What does God mean when He declares, "I'm going to put a hook in your jaw"? In the ancient world a master would take a stick with a hook on the end of it and insert it in the jaw of a donkey. This forced the animal to follow and obey. Through Ezekiel, God says, "Let Me tell you something, Russia. Let Me tell you something, Iran. Let Me tell you something, all you Islamic countries who want to destroy Israel. I'm in control of you, and when I'm ready, I'm going to put a hook in your jaw. I'm going to drag you down to the mountains of Israel, and then I'm going to kill you Myself on account of My people, Israel."

All these nations hate Israel. They have vowed to destroy her, but God will have an unmistakable response. These events could begin before the end of this day. All the nations Ezekiel lists are present and accounted for. They are all aligned and unified in their hatred of Israel. Nevertheless, God is also present and aware, and He will intervene with unrestrained ferocity.

THE COVENANT WITH THE ANTICHRIST

I believe Israel will soon confirm a seven-year covenant with the Antichrist. I believe this alliance could come in response to the Gog and Magog war.

The prophet Daniel wrote about the abomination of desolation:

> Then he shall confirm a covenant with many [Daniel is speaking of
> Israel] for one week [a week signifies seven years];
> But in the middle of the week [which indicates three and a half years
> into the seven year tribulation]
> He shall bring an end to sacrifice and offering.
> And on the wing of abominations shall be one who makes desolate,
> Even until the consummation, which is determined,
> Is poured out on the desolate (Daniel 9:27, commentary mine).

In Matthew 24, Jesus gives His own commentary to this passage from the book of Daniel:

> Therefore when you see the "abomination of desolation," spoken of by Daniel the prophet, standing in the holy place (whoever reads, let him understand), then let those who are in Judea flee to the mountains. Let him who is on the housetop not go down to take anything out of his house. And let him who is in the field not go back to get his clothes. But woe to those who are pregnant and to those who are nursing babies in those days! And pray that your flight may not be in winter or on the Sabbath. For then there will be great tribulation, such as has not been since the beginning of the world until this time, no, nor ever shall be. And unless those days were shortened, no flesh would be saved; but for the elect's sake those days will be shortened (Matthew 24:15–22).

Jesus is referring to the time of the Tribulation, the last seven years of human history. The Church will not be on earth at that time because Jesus will have already taken it to heaven with Him in the Rapture.

During the first three and a half years of the Tribulation, the Antichrist will come to power, and the Temple will be rebuilt in Israel. Then the Antichrist will enter the Temple, stop all sacrifices, and proclaim himself God. The Bible calls this "the abomination of desolation" (Daniel 11:31). The next three and a half years of the Tribulation will be the most severe time in human history. That is why Jesus says, "Unless those days were shortened, no flesh would be saved" (Matthew 24:22). The second half of the Tribulation is the Great Tribulation. Paul describes the same event:

> Let no one deceive you by any means; for *that Day will not come* unless the falling away comes first, and the man of sin [this is the Antichrist] is revealed, the son of perdition, who opposes and exalts himself above all that is called God or that is worshiped, so that he sits as God in the temple of God, showing himself that he is God (2 Thessalonians 2:3–4, commentary mine).

THE REBUILDING OF THE TEMPLE ON THE TEMPLE MOUNT

As I wrote previously, the blood moons of 1949 and 1950 followed the restoration of the Holy Land to the Jewish people. Then in 1967 the Holy City of Jerusalem was restored as well. A third event must happen for the abomination of desolation to occur: The Temple must be rebuilt in Jerusalem. The Jewish presence on the Temple Mount has increased dramatically over the past several years. But something has happened recently that hasn't occurred in nearly 2,000 years—Jews are now openly praying on the Temple Mount in full view of the police and the Muslims. According to *The Jerusalem Post,* while there has been no official change in the Israeli government's policy, Jews now pray there on a regular basis. Rabbi Eliyahu Weber is one of the people leading Jewish worshippers there. He said that he and his fellow worshippers deliberately conduct prayers there twice a day, although they do not try to cause a scene.

In the past, police would have ejected non-Muslims, but over time the policy has changed in practice, even though there has been no official modification. The number of Jews visiting the Temple Mount has almost tripled in the last five years. "The essence of our presence on the Temple Mount shows that this place belongs to the Jewish people," said Weber. "If we don't come, [it appears] that it doesn't interest us. The Temple Mount is ours, and we need to know the importance of being there."[37]

The final goal, however, is to rebuild the Temple, which *The Jerusalem Post* admits. This unprecedented construction is closer than you think. The Temple Institute, the Temple Mount Faithful, and other organizations have begun preparing for the construction and are intensifying their efforts.[38] What is happening at the Temple Mount is significant. It is one more step to fulfilling the Bible's prophecy.

What is the significance of the Temple Mount? Some Jews believe it is the site of the original Garden of Eden, including those who believe the location of the Church of the Holy Sepulchre is the burial site of Adam. A mere 36 acres, this small piece of land is one of the most important and most disputed properties in the world. If Jerusalem is the frontline for the end times, then the Temple Mount is ground zero for the fulfillment of Bible prophecy and will be the staging ground for the Battle of Armageddon. The Temple Mount is also the place to which Christ will return and the location of His throne during His millennial rule. Just as some believe human history began on this site, others believe the world will end here at the conclusion of Jesus' one-thousand-year rule when Satan will lead the nations of the world in an attempt to kill Jesus again. The apostle John writes:

> Now when the thousand years have expired, Satan will be released from his prison and will go out to deceive the nations which are in the four corners of the earth, Gog and Magog, to gather them together to battle, whose number *is* as the sand of the sea. They went up on the breadth of the earth and surrounded the camp of the saints and the beloved city. And fire came down from God out of heaven and devoured them (Revelation 20:7–8).

The Bible offers *four prophetic portraits of redemption* related to the Temple Mount:

1. On the Temple Mount, *Melchizedek* appeared as a type of Christ.

> Then Melchizedek king of Salem brought out bread and wine; he *was* the priest of God Most High. And he blessed him and said: "Blessed be Abram of God Most High, Possessor of heaven and earth; And blessed be God Most High, Who has delivered your enemies into your hand." And he gave him a tithe of all (Genesis 14:18–20).

The Bible provides no genealogy for Melchizedek, which means he was a king-priest with neither beginning nor end. He received tithes from Abraham and ministered blessing and peace to him. The writer of Hebrews says:

For this Melchizedek, king of Salem, priest of the Most High God, who met Abraham returning from the slaughter of the kings and blessed him, to whom also Abraham gave a tenth part of all, first being translated "king of righteousness," and then also king of Salem, meaning "king of peace," without father, without mother, without genealogy, having neither beginning of days nor end of life, but made like the Son of God, remains a priest continually. Now consider how great this man *was,* to whom even the patriarch Abraham gave a tenth of the spoils (Hebrews 7:1–4).

The Temple Mount first appears in the Bible with the arrival of Melchizedek. This amazing king-priest prophetically reveals to us the coming ministry of Jesus, *our Eternal King and High Priest.*

2. *Abraham offered up Isaac* on the Temple Mount. Another name for the Temple Mount is Mount Moriah, which means "Chosen by *Yahweh.*" Genesis gives this account:

Then they came to the place of which God had told him. And Abraham built an altar there and placed the wood in order; and he bound Isaac his son and laid him on the altar, upon the wood. And Abraham stretched out his hand and took the knife to slay his son. But the Angel of the LORD called to him from heaven and said, "Abraham, Abraham!" So he said, "Here I am." And He said, "Do not lay your hand on the lad, or do anything to him; for now I know that you fear God, since you have not withheld your son, your only *son,* from Me" (Genesis 22:9–12).

This encounter is another powerful prophetic portrait of God the Father willingly offering up His only Son as a sin offering for all humanity. In the end God provides a ram, which Abraham then gives back to God as his sacrifice. God, then, is the source of all our provision, *Yahweh Jireh* or the Lord our Provider.

3. King David purchased the Temple Mount from Ornan to build an altar. The reason David needed to build the altar was to stop the plague God had sent after David chose to take a census of the people. David decided to take the census to reassure himself that he had enough fighting men should he face an enemy. Up to this point in David's life, he had always relied on God to defend him, even against the great giant, Goliath. David forgot that God was the source of his defense rather than human soldiers or armaments. The Chronicler offers this account in 1 Chronicles chapter 21:

> Now Satan stood up against Israel, and moved David to number Israel. [Remember, this is David, the famed "giant killer."] (v. 1, commentary mine).

> So the LORD sent a plague upon Israel, and seventy thousand men of Israel fell. And God sent an angel to Jerusalem to destroy it. As he was destroying, the LORD looked and relented of the disaster, and said to the angel who was destroying, "It is enough; now restrain your hand." And the angel of the LORD stood by the threshing floor of Ornan the Jebusite. [Ornan's threshing floor is the site of the Temple Mount.] (vv. 14–15, commentary mine).

Then David said to Ornan, "Grant me the place of *this* thresh-ing floor, that I may build an altar on it to the LORD. You shall grant it to me at the full price, that the plague may be with-drawn from the people." But Ornan said to David, "Take *it* to yourself, and let my lord the king do *what is* good in his eyes. Look, I *also* give *you* the oxen for burnt offerings, the thresh-ing implements for wood, and the wheat for the grain offering; I give *it* all." Then King David said to Ornan, "No, but I will surely buy *it* for the full price, for I will not take what is yours for the LORD, nor offer burnt offerings with *that which* costs *me* nothing" (vv. 22–24).

And David built there an altar to the LORD, and offered burnt offerings and peace offerings, and called on the LORD; and He answered him from heaven by fire on the altar of burnt offer-ing. So the LORD commanded the angel, and he returned his sword to its sheath (vv. 26–27).

This chapter is a prophetic portrayal of Satan's strategy to tempt us to sin, which brings about destruction and, ultimately, death. However, God made the offering of Jesus' blood, which holds back God's wrath and reconciles us to Him so we can have peace with Him.

4. God charged Solomon to construct the Temple on the Temple Mount. Then Solomon dedicated it to the Lord. The Chronicler writes,

King Solomon offered a sacrifice of twenty-two thousand bulls and one hundred and twenty thousand sheep. So the king and all the people dedicated the house of God (2 Chronicles 7:5).

Solomon built the Temple according to the Lord's instructions and specifications so that it would match the real Temple, which is in heaven. In today's dollars this Temple would have cost billions of dollars. It was the place the Hebrew people were to offer lavish sacrifice and worship to God. Again, the Chronicler writes:

> Then the Lord appeared to Solomon by night, and said to him: "I have heard your prayer, and have chosen this place for Myself as a house of sacrifice. When I shut up heaven and there is no rain, or command the locusts to devour the land, or send pestilence among My people, if My people who are called by My name will humble themselves, and pray and seek My face, and turn from their wicked ways, then I will hear from heaven, and will forgive their sin and heal their land. Now My eyes will be open and My ears attentive to prayer made in this place. For now I have chosen and sanctified this house, that My name may be there forever; and My eyes and My heart will be there perpetually" (2 Chronicles 7:12–16).

The last verse in this passage has a dual meaning: God has chosen the Temple and the Temple Mount as a very special place on earth throughout all human history, and His eyes and heart are always there. God is saying He has a special awareness of this place, which holds deep emotion for Him. When Jesus died on the cross, the veil of the Temple was torn down the middle from top to bottom, and we became the Temple of the Holy Spirit. His eyes are now focused on us, and we are His eternal dwelling place. As you can see, the Temple and the Temple Mount are special places for God to interact with humanity.

The Temple Mount also plays a critical role for the future. According to the Bible, *four significant prophetic events* will take place on the Temple Mount, and I believe they will happen soon.

1. The Temple will be rebuilt on the Temple Mount. The apostle John delivers this prophetic word:

> Then I was given a reed like a measuring rod. And the angel stood, saying, "Rise and measure the temple of God, the altar, and those who worship there. But leave out the court which is outside the temple, and do not measure it, for it has been given to the Gentiles. And they will tread the holy city underfoot for forty-two months" (Revelation 11:1–2).

According to Daniel 9, the Antichrist will execute a seven-year covenant with Israel. As I see it right now, I believe the terms of this deal will give half of the Temple Mount to the Jews in exchange for half of the city of Jerusalem, which is what the Palestinians and the United Nations have been demanding. This Scripture passage makes that very clear, and the rebuilt Temple will also leave room for the Dome of the Rock to remain.

2. The two witnesses written about in Revelation 11 will minister for the first half of the Tribulation on the Temple Mount. I will discuss them more in length later, but I believe these two men are Enoch and Elijah. God will send them as His own personal emissaries to preach the absolute truth of His Word and to judge His enemies. They will be hated by almost everyone. John writes:

> And I will give power to my two witnesses, and they will prophesy one thousand two hundred and sixty days, clothed in sackcloth. These are the two olive trees and the two lampstands standing before the God of the earth. And if anyone wants to harm them, fire proceeds from their mouth and devours their enemies. And if anyone wants to harm them, he must be killed in this manner. These have power to shut heaven, so that no rain falls in the days of their prophecy; and they have power over waters to turn them to blood, and to strike the earth with all plagues, as often as they desire. When they finish their testimony, the beast that ascends out of the bottomless pit will make war against them, overcome them, and kill them. And their dead bodies will lie in the street of the great city which spiritually is called Sodom and Egypt, where also our Lord was crucified. Then those from the peoples, tribes, tongues, and nations will see their dead bodies three-and-a-half days, and not allow their dead bodies to be put into graves. And those who dwell on the earth will rejoice over them, make merry, and send gifts to one another, because these two prophets tormented those who dwell on the earth. Now after the three-and-a-half days the breath of life from God entered them, and they stood on their feet, and great fear fell on those who saw them. And they heard a loud voice from heaven saying to them, "Come up here." And they ascended to heaven in a cloud, and their enemies saw them. In the same hour there was a great earthquake, and a tenth of the city fell. In the earthquake seven thousand people were killed, and the rest were afraid and gave glory to the God of heaven (Revelation 11:3–13).

3. The Antichrist will proclaim himself "God" there. He will enter the rebuilt Temple three and one-half years into the seven-year Tribulation, and there he will blaspheme God. This event will signal the Great Tribulation, which is the second half of the Tribulation. Daniel prophesied about this event in Daniel 9, and Jesus spoke of it in Matthew 24. John also writes:

> And he was given a mouth speaking great things and blasphemies, and he was given authority to continue for forty-two months. Then he opened his mouth in blasphemy against God, to blaspheme His name, His tabernacle, and those who dwell in heaven (Revelation 13:5–6).

4. Jesus will return with us and establish His millennial throne in the Temple on the Temple Mount. The prophet Zechariah writes about this event:

> Then the LORD will go forth
> And fight against those nations,
> As He fights in the day of battle.
> And in that day His feet will stand on the Mount of Olives,
> Which faces Jerusalem on the east.
> And the Mount of Olives shall be split in two,
> From east to west,
> *Making* a very large valley;
> Half of the mountain shall move toward the north
> And half of it toward the south.
> Then you shall flee *through* My mountain valley,
> For the mountain valley shall reach to Azal.
> Yes, you shall flee

As you fled from the earthquake
In the days of Uzziah king of Judah.
Thus the LORD my God will come,
And all the saints with You.
It shall come to pass in that day
That there will be no light;
The lights will diminish.
It shall be one day
Which is known to the LORD—
Neither day nor night.
But at evening time it shall happen
That it will be light.
And in that day it shall be
That living waters shall flow from Jerusalem,
Half of them toward the eastern sea
And half of them toward the western sea;
In both summer and winter it shall occur.
And the LORD shall be King over all the earth.
In that day it shall be—
"The Lord *is* one,"
And His name one (Zechariah 14:3–9).

The apostle John then writes this parallel text about the same event:

Now I saw heaven opened, and behold, a white horse. And He who sat on him *was* called Faithful and True, and in righteousness He judges and makes war. His eyes *were* like a flame of fire, and on His head *were* many crowns. He had a name written that no one knew except Himself. He *was* clothed with a robe dipped in blood, and

His name is called The Word of God. And the armies in heaven, clothed in fine linen, white and clean, followed Him on white horses. Now out of His mouth goes a sharp sword, that with it He should strike the nations. And He Himself will rule them with a rod of iron. He Himself treads the winepress of the fierceness and wrath of Almighty God. And He has on *His* robe and on His thigh a name written:

KING OF KINGS AND
LORD OF LORDS.

Then I saw an angel standing in the sun; and he cried with a loud voice, saying to all the birds that fly in the midst of heaven, "Come and gather together for the supper of the great God, that you may eat the flesh of kings, the flesh of captains, the flesh of mighty men, the flesh of horses and of those who sit on them, and the flesh of all *people,* free and slave, both small and great." And I saw the beast, the kings of the earth, and their armies, gathered together to make war against Him who sat on the horse and against His army (Revelation 19:11–19).

This final event ends human history as we know it and ushers in the one-thousand-year rule of Christ. The Church, the bride of Christ, will rule and reign with Him during this time. Jesus will rule the earth from the Temple Mount. I remind you again that the Temple Mount is *ground zero* for human history. And the start of these events is falling into place right now. It is in the news daily and continues to intensify.

And it is more proof that our God is in control and our Bible tells the future in advance. For believers, the future couldn't be brighter. We will not be here for the horrific events that will happen during the Tribulation. We will be at the Marriage Supper of the Lamb with Jesus. And we will be at His side as He returns to rule the earth as King of Kings and Lord of Lords.

JESUS WILL RULE THE EARTH
FROM THE TEMPLE MOUNT.

ASTRONOMICAL SIGNS
AT A TIPPING POINT

4

WHAT DO THE "LIGHT THINGS" SAY?

Here is what Genesis tells us about the time God made the sun, moon, and stars when He created the universe:

> Then God said, "Let there be lights in the firmament of the heavens to divide the day from the night; and **let them be for signs and seasons**, and for days and years; and let them be for lights in the firmament of the heavens to give light on the earth"; and it was so (Genesis 1:14–15, emphasis added).

This passage contains a very important concept in the Hebrew language that is usually not translated into English. When God says, "Let there be lights" the word for "lights" (*haower*) literally means *'light things.'* The reason this word is so significant is that the God of Israel wants people to know that these lights are only "things" and not deities. He is the only God, and the lights are His instruments, used for His purposes. They otherwise have no power, and they certainly aren't gods, like the pagan people surrounding Israel thought. As this passage of Scripture notes, one of the major reasons God created the sun, moon, and stars was for signs and seasons. They are God's "things" to tell us what

He is doing. The word translated "sign" is derived from the word *owth,* which means 'to signal, warn, or give an omen.' The word translated "season" is drawn from the word *moed,* which means 'feast or appointed season.' So, God created the sun, moon, and stars as signals in the sky to establish His time clock for the feasts of Israel and as signs of important events.

For example, God used the stars as a sign and season announcing the birth of Jesus. The wise men from the east used a star to guide them to Him. Interestingly enough, these foreigners had more discernment about the signs in the heavens than any of the Jews. These travelers had studied astronomy and understood how God speaks through the heavenly bodies.

Just as God announced Christ's first coming in the skies, so He will also announce the Second Coming. In an earlier chapter I discussed how the blood moons foretell events of the end times, but those are not the only signs in the skies. Jesus Himself spoke about the way God would use the signs in the heavens to signal end times events. For example, in the gospel of Luke, Jesus prophesied His own return:

> And there will be signs in the sun, in the moon, and in the stars; and on the earth distress of nations, with perplexity, the sea and the waves roaring; men's hearts failing them from fear and the expectation of those things which are coming on the earth, for the powers of the heavens will be shaken. Then they will see the Son of Man coming in a cloud with power and great glory. Now when these things begin to happen, look up and lift up your heads, because your redemption draws near (Luke 21:25–28).

Apart from Jesus' return, every part of that prophecy has been fulfilled or is in the process of being fulfilled as the conditions of the earth continue to worsen. We have also seen amazing and miraculous signs in the sun, moon, and stars just as Jesus said we would just prior to His return.

Over time, I have noticed two major problems with how Bible prophecy is handled by Christians. First, some Christians have a tendency to exaggerate events, or they even make up prophetic notions that don't actually exist. You have probably heard of certain individuals setting very specific dates when they insist particular prophetic events will happen. In virtually every case where this occurs, they are proven to be wrong, and they lose credibility. I am confident of the things I preach and teach, but I am not God. I believe the wisest approach is to point to the signs and evidences but let God measure time and keep the dates.

The second problem is that some well-meaning Christians ignore clear evidence and important signs. They are unaware of the actions God is taking, or they dismiss signs and events because they don't want to be seen as alarmist or unreliable. I must tell you that I believe neither of these two extremes are wise. Remember, the people of God missed the first coming of the Messiah, even though they had direct evidence from the Scriptures and God even announced it in the sky. Christians who follow either of these two streams of thought may be altogether reliable on other matters about the Bible, but they miss a great opportunity to encourage other believers and warn unbelievers.

I make this statement because as I said before, I believe we are living in the last days prior to the return of Jesus. I don't know exactly when He is coming, but I see all the signs and symptoms, and I want as many people to be as ready as possible.

Along with the information I have already given about blood moons, I would like you to know about two additional astronomical events that I believe have great significance for the end times. They don't tell us exactly when Jesus will return, but they get us much closer than we would be if we ignored them.

THE CROSSING ECLIPSES

In 2017 the US experienced two major natural events within a single week. On Monday, August 21, a total solar eclipse crossed over the US in a band that spanned the entire contiguous nation, passing from the Pacific to the Atlantic coasts. This astrological phenomenon had not happened for 99 years, although it will occur again on April 8, 2024. When that event takes place, the eclipse will mark an "X" over the US. Historically, Jewish tradition considers solar eclipses to be warnings to the world and lunar eclipses to be warnings to Israel. Consequently, Jews have kept both a lunar and a solar calendar. Given that tradition, are these two crossing eclipses a warning for the world? I believe they very well could be.

———————— • ————————

GOD CREATED THE SUN, MOON,
AND STARS AS SIGNALS IN
THE SKY TO ESTABLISH HIS
TIME CLOCK FOR THE FEASTS
OF ISRAEL AND AS SIGNS OF
IMPORTANT EVENTS.

Let me take you to the year 1918. The last full continental eclipse of this type occurred on June 8 of that year. You see, most eclipses fall directly over water or other unpopulated areas. World War I began on July 28, 1914, but the US had only recently joined in the conflict by declaring war on Germany on April 6, 1917. Large numbers of soldiers in the American Expeditionary Forces on the Western front under the command of General John Joseph "Black Jack" Pershing arrived in France very early in the summer of 1918. Then the eclipse occurred on June 8 and cut across the entire continental US.

By the autumn of 1918, the Americans had brought the Allies closer to victory, but the fighting continued. Soldiers hunkered down in the trenches amid deplorable conditions. As if that was not bad enough, an epidemic that first appeared to be the common cold began spreading through Europe. However, it was far more than a cold. Over a span of two years, the Spanish flu infected one out of every five people in the world. It was most deadly for people between the ages of 20 and 40—the age of fighting men. It reached around the globe, ultimately infecting 28 percent of Americans. At the end of the epidemic, approximately 675,000 people died from the flu in the US. While the war raged in Europe, half of the soldiers died from the flu rather than through enemy combat. The flu felled 43,000 American military personnel. In retrospect, the flu was the greatest factor in the war and hastened its end. In fact, it killed more people than the war itself, as many as 40 million. Epidemiologists have speculated on the origins of the outbreak with no success.[39] Was the 1918 eclipse a sign of things to come? Personally, I believe it was.

Before 1918 the last time a solar eclipse spanned the entire US was on November 30, 1776.[40] If you are an American, I don't need to remind you of the significance of that year. The eclipse of 2017 was the first time for most living Americans, except those who were nearing the age of 100 and above, to witness a continental eclipse. It was the most-viewed eclipse in human history. It first made landfall in the continental US near the city of Salem, Oregon, at exactly sunset time in Jerusalem. So technically, as the sun disappeared in America, it also set in Jerusalem.[41] Salem is also the name of the location where Abraham met Melchizedek and the current site of the city of Jerusalem. The name Jerusalem comes from the combination of the prefix *jeru-* ("city of") and the noun *salem* ("peace").

On August 25, 2017, only five days after the eclipse, Hurricane Harvey made landfall along the Texas coast, near Rockport and Port Aransas, which comes from the Basque phrase, *Aranza zu,* based on a phrase said by a shepherd in 1740. According to the legend, the Virgin Mary appeared in a vision while the shepherd tended sheep in the field. The shepherd said, *"Aranzan zu,"* meaning "You are sitting in thorns." This vision became known as "The Lady of Aranzazu" or "Our Lady of Thorns."[42] Indeed, the entire Gulf Coast was "sitting in thorns" as catastrophic flooding soon overtook many coastal cities.

Port Aransas, however, was not in the original landfall predictions from the National Weather Service. Instead, Corpus Christi, Texas, appeared to be in the direct path of Harvey. When landfall finally happened at 10 pm on the 25th, the hurricane had missed the city. *Corpus Christi* is derived from a Latin term that means "body of Christ." Was this a sign? I believe it could be. The wrath of God will come in its fullness during the Great Tribulation, but the body of Christ, the Church, will miss the coming terror in the same way Noah and Lot escaped the wrath of God and the destruction that was to come. Believers will be caught up in the Rapture. During the Tribulation, they will be marrying Jesus and feasting with Him at the Marriage Supper of the Lamb. Those who remain on earth will be sitting in the thorns.

The next solar eclipse will cross the continental US a mere seven years after the 2017 event on April 8, 2024. Its crossing point will mark an "X" over the US. The combined time for the total eclipse will be seven minutes. The exact point of the crossing will be in the little village of Makanda, Illinois, on Salem Road—note Salem *again*. This area of southern Illinois was once called "Little Egypt." The small town of Makanda is known by the nickname "Star of Egypt." Incidentally, this was also the crossing path for the 2017 Eclipse. The Star of Egypt had a long history in Egyptian mythology and has been identified as the star Sirius. Throughout Christian history Sirius has often been identified as the star the wisemen observed on their travels to see the newborn King Jesus in Bethlehem.[43] This connection is, of course, speculative. But isn't it interesting that the Star of Egypt may have heralded the first coming of the Messiah, and the 2024 eclipse will cross directly over the "Star of Egypt"?

Perhaps all of these connections are mere coincidences, but how many coincidences signify something is happening like has never happened before? Eclipses rarely cross in the exact same location, except one will in 2024. Right before the full totality of the eclipse, the sun will look like a diamond wedding ring in the sky. I do not know if these events herald the Second Coming of the Lord, but I am paying close attention.

THE REVELATION 12 SIGN

I must tell you before I discuss the next astronomical sign that I believe this is the *second-most significant event* related to the end times of my lifetime. As I said before, I consider Jerusalem falling under Jewish control in 1967 as the most significant event. In 2017 an astronomical sign occurred. This is not a common event. Although various parts of this astronomical event have occurred in recorded history, they have never *all* happened at the same time. Here is the description of this end times sign in Revelation:

> **Now a great sign appeared in heaven: a woman clothed with the sun, with the moon under her feet, and on her head a garland of twelve stars.** Then being with child, she cried out in labor

and in pain to give birth. And another sign appeared in heaven: behold, a great, fiery red dragon having seven heads and ten horns, and seven diadems on his heads. His tail drew a third of the stars of heaven and threw them to the earth. And the dragon stood before the woman who was ready to give birth, to devour her Child as soon as it was born. She bore a male Child who was to rule all nations with a rod of iron. And her Child was caught up to God and His throne. Then the woman fled into the wilderness, where she has a place prepared by God, that they should feed her there one thousand two hundred and sixty days (Revelation 12:1–6, emphasis added).

On September 23, 2017, viewed most clearly from the city of Jerusalem, the constellation Leo was positioned directly above the head of the constellation Virgo, the "virgin." (This event can be viewed through the open-source Stellarium Astronomy Software at www.stellarium.org or search for "Revelation 12 Sign" on YouTube.) This event coincided with the High Holy Days of Rosh Hoshana, also known as the Feast of Trumpets. The constellation Leo is outlined by nine bright stars, although it contains many stars. The planets Mercury, Venus, and Mars joined these brighter stars to make the appearance of a 12-jeweled crown sitting atop Virgo's head. Virgo was *clothed with the sun* as the sun stood at her shoulder. The moon was also beneath her, *"under her feet."*

"Then being with child, she cried out in labor and in pain to give birth." The planet Jupiter takes its name from the king of the Roman gods, who is the same character as the Greek god

Zeus. Known as "The King Planet," Jupiter is often associated by the Jews with the Messiah. The planet entered the constellation's "womb" on November 20, 2016, and retrograded from February through July of 2017. It exited the "womb" on September 9, 2017, which means Jupiter spent 41 weeks inside Virgo, which is roughly the duration of a normal human gestation. Jupiter exited through the east end of Virgo, as if leaving from between her feet. Before Jupiter's retrograde, the Comet Borisov, which has been called "the Conception Comet," traveled from the "loins" of the constellation Leo and entered the "womb" of constellation Virgo on November 17, 2016. This was Comet Borisov's only trip it will make through our solar system because it is not solar orbital. Not only has Jupiter been called "The King Planet," but it is also the largest, "ruling all others." *"She bore a male Child who was to rule all nations with a rod of iron."*

"And another sign appeared in heaven: behold, a great, fiery red dragon having seven heads and ten horns, and seven diadems on his heads. His tail drew a third of the stars of heaven and threw them to the earth. And the dragon stood before the woman who was ready to give birth, to devour her Child as soon as it was born." Where, then, was the "great, fiery red dragon"? During this event a fiery object appeared between the constellation Virgo's legs as she "gave birth" to Jupiter. This incident was seen by several observers and recorded by sky-watching websites. However, it was quickly redacted by Google and NASA. Why did this happen? Someone has the answer, but its disappearance is cause for reasonable speculation.[44]

As soon as the woman in Revelation chapter 12 gives birth, Satan and his angels are cast out of heaven. God will not allow Satan to "crash" the Marriage Supper of the Lamb. Then in Revelation chapter 13, the Antichrist rises out of the sea and begins his tyrannical rule. In Revelation chapter 14, God commissions 144,000 Jews to preach the gospel to the world. So, Revelation chapter 12 ushers in a series of events that will finally bring about the millennial rule of Christ.

KEEP YOUR EYES ON THE STARS

I'm going to close this chapter by quoting someone who was not a Bible scholar or theologian at all, but his saying is true. When I was an older teen, Casey Kasem, along with Don Bustany, Tom Rounds, and Ron Jacobs, created a weekly radio music countdown program entitled "American Top 40." Teens all over America would listen eagerly for several hours for Kasem to reveal the number one song of the week. For the next 39 years until his retirement, Kasem ended every show he hosted with the same sage advice: "Keep your eyes on the stars and your feet on the ground!" I'm not Casey Kasem, and he was no pastor, but I would give you very similar advice: watch the signs in the skies but stay firmly grounded.

Be alert to the signs but remember that signs are not events themselves; rather, they point to future events. The two events I have described in this chapter are some of the most amazing events in my lifetime. I believe they signaled to Christians things that will happen in the very near future related to the Church, Israel, and the rest of the world. None of these signs give the full picture, but taken together, they get us closer to seeing what God is doing.

TRUTH AT A TIPPING POINT

5

TRUTH ON LIFE SUPPORT

Unless you've been living in a cave, forest, or somewhere else off the grid, you have recognized the moral changes taking place in our nation. We are experiencing a dramatic falling away from traditional values and biblical morality. This current state of affairs should not be a surprise to you. What may be news to you, though, is that the Bible prophesies about this contemporary situation and tells us that it is one of the major signs of the end times.

In the book of 1 Thessalonians, the apostle Paul addresses the return of Christ in every chapter. In the fourth chapter, he gives the Bible's clearest description of the Rapture of the Church. The Bible doesn't specifically use the word "rapture," but it does contain the concept. Rapture comes from the Latin word *rapturo*, which means 'to seize hastily; to snatch away.' The Greek word from which we get the concept of rapture is *harpazo*, and it is found in Paul's first letter to the Thessalonians. The Rapture will be when Jesus returns, and believers who are alive will be taken up with Him. This group of people will never die, which means if you're alive and saved when Jesus comes, then you will not see death.

Preceding the current generation, all the people who ever lived eventually died, with just two exceptions—Enoch and Elijah. I mentioned them earlier and will discuss these two biblical men later, but other than them, everyone died. However, there will be another group of people who won't experience death: those who are believers on earth when Jesus returns. I want to be among those people who will be caught up with Jesus and taken directly to heaven. I don't want to have to go to the grave to get there, and the Bible says some of us won't have to do that.

Paul describes the moment when Jesus returns to rapture His Church:

> For this we say to you by the word of the Lord, that we who are alive *and* remain until the coming of the Lord will by no means precede those who are asleep. For the Lord Himself will descend from heaven with a shout, with the voice of an archangel, and with the trumpet of God. And the dead in Christ will rise first. **Then we who are alive *and* remain shall be caught up together with them in the clouds to meet the Lord in the air**. And thus we will always be with the Lord. Therefore comfort one another with these words (1 Thessalonians 4:15–18, emphasis added).

In an instant believers will go from here on earth directly into the presence of Jesus in the skies. This is how the Rapture will happen, and I believe it may come at any moment. It's one of the next major prophetic events that will occur in the world.

You may think Paul's words to the Thessalonians would have comforted them, but it actually upset a lot of people in that local church. How do we know this? Because after he wrote the first letter, a rumor was being circulated that the Rapture had already come and Jesus had left the Thessalonians behind. You can imagine how much that would disturb them. What if Jesus came and He didn't choose you to go with Him? It's an upsetting thought, right? Paul knew it was necessary to write another letter, so he penned his Second Letter to the Thessalonians and sent it only a few weeks after the first one.

THREE SCENES OF THE END TIMES

In 2 Thessalonians, Paul offers comfort to the believers in Thessalonica's church. He is telling them, "Let me be clear—Jesus hasn't come yet, nor have you been left behind." Paul provides a clear and graphic panoramic view of how the world will appear at the return of Christ. Consider three distinct scenes of the end times Paul describes in 2 Thessalonians 2.

Scene 1: The Great Falling Away and the Arrival of the Antichrist

In Paul's first scene people are in direct rebellion against God. The "man of sin"—the Antichrist—appears, and he is ready to lead the world. I believe this scene is happening even as I write these words. This is what Paul says:

> Now, brethren, concerning the coming of our Lord Jesus Christ and our gathering together to Him, we ask you, not to be soon shaken in mind or troubled, either by spirit or by word or by letter, as if from us, as though the day of Christ had come. Let no one deceive you by any means; for that Day [Paul is referring to the day Jesus returns.] *will not come* unless the falling away [The Greek word Paul uses is *apostasia,* which is the root of the word apostasy.] comes first, and the man of sin is revealed, the son of perdition, who opposes and exalts himself above all that is called God or that is worshiped, so that he sits as God in the temple of God, showing himself that he is God (2 Thessalonians 2:1–4, commentary mine).

Once again Paul is reminding the Thessalonians that the Second Coming of Christ has not yet happened. He then tells them that Jesus will not return until there is a worldwide falling away from truth. This apostasy will be a widespread rejection of biblical Christianity, including both theology and morality.

The title "antichrist" isn't used often in the Scripture. In fact, only the apostle John uses it as a title for a person. However, the Bible uses many names to describe the Antichrist; some Bible scholars have listed as many as 38 names. Some of these names may refer directly to Satan or another historic figure under the influence of the devil, but there's good reason to believe that many or all of them refer to the Antichrist:

- The man of the earth (Psalm 10:18)

- The mighty man (Psalm 52:1)

- The adversary (Psalm 74:10)

- The king of Assyria (Isaiah 10:12)

- The little horn (Daniel 7:8)

- The prince who is to come (Daniel 9:26)

- A vile person (Daniel 11:21)

- The king (Daniel 11:36)

- The worthless shepherd (Zechariah 11:16–17)

- The man of sin, the son of perdition (2 Thessalonians 2:3–4)

- The beast (Revelation 11:7)

This is quite a list, but even it is not complete. Nevertheless, as you can see, the concept and person of the Antichrist is prevalent throughout the Bible. In all instances these titles have one common theme—*deception*. If I were to say a man was "anti," what would that imply? It can mean he is against or opposed to something. But it can also mean that he replaces something or offers himself instead of it. In the case of the Antichrist, he will present himself to the world as the alternative to Christ, and through his deception, many will believe and follow him.

---●---

IF YOU'RE ALIVE AND SAVED
WHEN JESUS COMES, THEN
YOU WILL NOT SEE DEATH.

In 2 Thessalonians 2:8 Paul calls the Antichrist "the lawless one," which is in keeping with the many other biblical names for this individual. The Greek word Paul uses that is translated as "lawless" is the word *anomia*. The word is used 13 times in the New Testament. It describes the condition of being without the law. Sometimes the word is used to describe someone who is ignorant of the law, but usually it describes someone who willfully violates it. In this verse Paul is describing someone who knowingly and intentionally opposes God's law, or someone who opposes God's Word as we know it in the Bible. As a consequence this person directly disobeys God and the Word, which is Jesus Christ (John 1).

Many people will be antichrists with a little "a," but only one will be the Antichrist with a capital "A." All of them will oppose Christ in one way or another, but this man will be diametrically opposed to God and His Son, Jesus Christ. In fact, we could say he will be Satan incarnate. He will be antithetical to the Word of God. The Antichrist will tell people that he is "God" incarnate and offer himself as the replacement for Jesus Christ, but he will really be Satan incarnate and a counterfeit messiah. Everything he will do will be in partnership with Satan himself, including presenting himself at Jerusalem's Temple Mount.

I believe we are seeing the world right now moving quickly toward the day when the Antichrist will make himself known. Satan will never win, but he is always working against God. He has a strategy to pour out his deception and thus prepare the world for an all-out rebellion against God. He is preparing the way for the Antichrist, much like John the Baptist prepared the way for Jesus by preaching repentance. Satan is doing the opposite by deceiving people with the ideas that sin is not real and there is no need to fear God. As it is today, his strategy has had great success. Here's an important text from the book of Psalms that talks about a worldwide rebellion against God in the end times:

> Why do the nations rage,
> And the people plot a vain thing?
> The kings of the earth set themselves,
> And the rulers take counsel together,
> Against the LORD and against His Anointed, *saying,*
> "Let us break Their bonds in pieces
> And cast away Their cords from us."
> He who sits in the heavens shall laugh;
> The Lord shall hold them in derision.
> Then He shall speak to them in His wrath,
> And distress them in His deep displeasure:
> "Yet I have set My King
> On My holy hill of Zion."
> "I will declare the decree:
> The LORD has said to Me,
> 'You *are* My Son,
> Today I have begotten You.
> Ask of Me, and I will give *You*
> The nations *for* Your inheritance,
> And the ends of the earth *for* Your possession.

You shall break them with a rod of iron;
You shall dash them to pieces like a potter's vessel.'"
Now therefore, be wise, O kings;
Be instructed, you judges of the earth.
Serve the LORD with fear,
And rejoice with trembling.
Kiss the Son, lest He be angry,
And you perish *in* the way,
When His wrath is kindled but a little.
Blessed *are* all those who put their trust in Him (Psalm 2:1–12).

As the world's people rage against God and scoff at the Lordship of Jesus Christ, God laughs at them. He declares to them that His Son will inherit the earth and reign from Jerusalem's Temple Mount, Mount Zion. Jesus will hold in His hand a rod of iron and rule for a millennium. God is warning the people and rulers of the world that they should kiss the Son (submit to His rule), or He will visit them with His wrath.

The apostle John writes about this outpouring of wrath:

I looked when He opened the sixth seal, and behold, there was a great earthquake; and the sun became black as sackcloth of hair, and the moon became like blood. And the stars of heaven fell to the earth, as a fig tree drops its late figs when it is shaken by a mighty wind. Then the sky receded as a scroll when it is rolled up, and every mountain and island was moved out of its place. And the kings of the earth, the great men, the rich men, the commanders, the mighty men, every slave and every free man, hid themselves in the caves and in the rocks of the mountains, and said to the mountains and rocks, "Fall on us and hide us from the face of Him who sits on the throne and from the wrath of the Lamb! For the great day of His wrath has come, and who is able to stand?" (Revelation 6:12–17).

As I write repeatedly in this book, believers will not be here for this event because just prior to the Antichrist entering the stage, Jesus will come and rapture His Bride, the Church. However, before Jesus comes, lawlessness will grow more and more until the time is ripe for Jesus to return and the "lawless one" will then enter the scene. He will lead the world to mock God, rebel against Him, and arrogantly defy Him. I believe that this time is very near.

One of the reasons I say the end is so close is because of the moral and spiritual condition of our present society. When I was growing up, the world was much different than what my grandchildren are experiencing right now. In my public school we began with daily prayer in the name of Jesus, and the Ten Commandments were posted on the walls of our classrooms. In fact, these things happened in almost every public school in the US at the time. Some of my readers will be able to attest to these facts. Most of us simply assumed our neighbors were Christians, although they may have attended different churches. Our teachers were almost always Christians. It was just that kind of world.

On June 25, 1962, the United States Supreme Court decided in the case of *Engel v. Vitale* that a prayer approved by the New York Board of Regents for use in schools violated the First

Amendment and constituted an establishment of religion.[45] The next year, the Court disallowed daily Bible readings in the case of *Abington School District v. Schempp* following a similar rationale.[46] These two landmark decisions ushered in a new "normal" in American public life and changed the face of our society. By 1980 few legal experts were surprised at the case of *Stone v. Graham*, in which the Court ruled that a Kentucky law requiring the posting of the Ten Commandments on the wall of every public school classroom was also found to be in violation of the First Amendment.[47] What may have seemed insignificant to casual observers quickly turned into a wholesale rejection of biblical morality within our society. We are living in a postmodern, post-Christian, and post-Bible culture. But it hasn't stopped there. The authority of Scripture is under attack, even from the inside of many churches. Little by little, cultural forces have joined in an all-out attack on everything the Bible teaches.

Many people are increasingly claiming the Bible contains "hate speech." Atheism is rising each year. In the past few years, a new religious status has grown significantly in the US, made up of people who check "none" on surveys that ask for religious affiliation. A 2013 Harris Poll found that 23 percent of all Americans have forsaken religion altogether, which was a dramatic increase from a 2007 poll that found only 12 percent of Americans who made the same claim.[48] The results are even higher for younger generations. A 2015 Pew Research Center poll found that 34–36 percent of millennials claim no religious affiliation.[49] In raw numbers 55.8 million US citizens see no purpose for religion in their lives.[50] Worldwide percentages are even more stark. While 71 percent of Americans still claim to be Christians, the number is shrinking.[51] What we've seen in the world in the last two decades is the result of a drift that began about 50 years ago, and it's picking up steam. We are witnessing a worldwide shift toward apostasy and a rejection of Jewish and Christian morality based on the Bible. In times past atheism and agnosticism hid in the shadows; today, they are blatantly out in the open.

Even more shocking, we are witnessing a similar drift in the Church, but we should not be caught completely by surprise. Jesus prophesied these circumstances would happen. He told His disciples that before He returned, one-half of the Church would become a false church. In Matthew 24:3 the disciples approached Jesus and asked Him, "What *will* be the sign of Your coming, and of the end of the age?" He replied, "Take heed that no one deceives you" (v. 4). Then He gave a graphic description that portrays the current circumstances in our world—the world at the end.

Next, in Matthew chapter 25, Jesus told two parables and a true story about His return and how His followers should prepare for it. The first parable is about 10 virgins. It is in this parable that Jesus prophesied about the falling away of half the Church:

Then the kingdom of heaven shall be likened to ten virgins who took their lamps and went out to meet the bridegroom. Now five of them were wise, and five *were* foolish. Those who *were* foolish took their lamps and took no oil with them, but the wise took oil in their vessels with their lamps. But while the bridegroom was delayed, they all slumbered and slept.

And at midnight a cry was *heard:* "Behold, the bridegroom is coming; go out to meet him!" Then all those virgins arose and trimmed their lamps. And the foolish said to the wise, 'Give us *some* of your oil, for our lamps are going out.' But the wise answered, saying, *'No,* lest there should not be enough for us and you; but go rather to those who sell, and buy for yourselves.' And while they went to buy, the bridegroom came, and those who were ready went in with him to the wedding; and the door was shut.

Afterward the other virgins came also, saying, "Lord, Lord, open to us!" But he answered and said, "Assuredly, I say to you, I do not know you."

Watch therefore, for you know neither the day nor the hour in which the Son of Man is coming (Matthew 25:1–13).

Notice Jesus didn't say we wouldn't know the season at all. He didn't say we wouldn't know the signs of the times. He simply said, "You won't know the day or the hour." There are 10 virgins and one bridegroom in this parable. The bridegroom represents Jesus, and the 10 virgins are symbolic of the Church in the world. Jesus effectively says, "When I come, only half of the Church will be prepared for My return. These believers will have their lamps trimmed."

Ships at sea used to have certain sailors assigned to trim lamps. That means they maintained the oil lights as a full-time job. When the lamps are a ship's only source of light at night, keeping them in working order is critical. The five wise virgins have been maintaining their lamps, and they will be ready when the bridegroom returns. However, the other half of the Church will be caught off guard. They won't see or recognize the Lord when He returns. Jesus is saying that half of the people who identify themselves as His followers won't even know Him when He comes back.

Did you know this situation is happening right before our eyes in the Church? Follow the news about churches across the US, and you will see that many have openly rejected the clear teachings of the Bible. Entire denominations have become "prochoice" (pro-abortion) and now funnel significant funds to abortion providers. On June 26, 2015, the US Supreme Court held in *Obergefell v. Hodges* that all states must grant same-sex marriages and recognize same-sex marriages granted by other states.[52] This decision came after protracted efforts by gay rights organizations to receive legal recognition of same-sex marriages. Although many Christian groups fought these efforts for years, the reality of the decision sunk in quickly. However, the Court did not and cannot compel churches to recognize or perform these marriages. Even so, growing numbers of congregations have ordained practicing homosexuals, and some groups have chosen practicing homosexuals as their top denominational leaders. Several denominations actively promote same-sex weddings and marriages. This issue is dividing American congregations and denominations right down the middle.

Many churches no longer believe in the inerrancy or authority of Scripture. Multitudes of those same churches no longer believe in an actual hell or the devil. Consider this: if the Bible is lying to us about hell, why would you think it's telling us the truth about heaven? If one thing in God's Word is wrong, then how can we trust anything it has to say? Do you realize Jesus taught more about hell than He did about heaven? Do we think Jesus is a liar? Would He, of all people, know what He is talking about? Some churches no longer believe what Jesus taught, but I am proclaiming to you right now: *the devil is real, and there is an actual, literal hell.* I am saying these things because the Bible is completely and absolutely inspired and infallible, and it is the Holy Word of God. Even more, Jesus knows what He's talking about! That you can believe.

Many churches today have embraced universalism. This false teaching has even crept into some Evangelical churches. Universalism says that Jesus is not the only way to heaven. In fact, you don't even need to consider heaven, because God is going to give it to you anyway, no matter what you do or believe. No particular religion will get you there. You can go if you're a good person, but you can also go if you're just a so-so person. Grace, faith, and the blood of Jesus have nothing to do with it.

A few years ago one of our board members for Marriage-Today went to a denominational meeting. He is a pastor of a church in a very large denomination. At this meeting, one of the denominational leaders said this: "I will not define my lifestyle or my sexuality by the four narrow corners of this Book [as he held up a Bible]. It is time for another testament to be written that is more up-to-date and written for the times in which we are living." As he finished, the crowd responded with thunderous applause. The majority of the people at the meeting seemed to agree with the speaker's sentiments. My friend reported, "I was absolutely stunned that anyone would have agreed with that statement." Nevertheless, this scene is happening in churches and denominations all over America.

Don't mistake what I am saying here. Many churches have held fast to the truth. They love Jesus and are living in eager anticipation of His return. But what we are seeing in many other churches and denominations is a bold rejection of the clear teachings of the Bible. So, I am echoing the apostle Paul here by saying, "Listen, dear believers. No, Jesus has not yet returned, and He won't come back until there's great apostasy—a great falling away—from the truth." I am telling you right now that we are witnessing this apostasy in our current time, right in front of our eyes. Jesus prophesied, "When I return, half of the Church will be false. Half of the Church will fall away. And I will not recognize them as Mine. They only pretend to know Me, but they don't truly know or follow Me." Again, I do not know the exact time when Jesus is coming, but I see the signs. The Bible describes the condition of the world to which Jesus will return, and this world looks a whole lot like that one.

Very soon after the Rapture, the Antichrist will reveal himself to the world, and the people of earth will worship him. He will confirm a seven-year covenant with Israel, which will signal the beginning of the Tribulation. In the middle of those years, he will proclaim himself as "God." The prophet Daniel writes:

> Then he shall confirm a covenant with many for one week;
> But in the middle of the week
> He shall bring an end to sacrifice and offering.
> And on the wing of abominations shall be one who makes desolate,
> Even until the consummation, which is determined,
> Is poured out on the desolate (Daniel 9:27).

The apostle John also gives this account of that time:

> He was granted *power* to give breath to the image of the beast, that the image of the beast should both speak and cause as many as would not worship the image of the beast to be killed. He causes all, both small and great, rich and poor, free and slave, to receive a mark on their right hand or on their foreheads, and that no one may buy or sell except one who has the mark or the name of the beast, or the number of his name (Revelation 13:15–17).

During the Tribulation the people on earth will have only two choices: worship the Antichrist or *die!* Those who take his mark and worship him, however, will be sentenced to hell for eternity. The world is gearing up for that moment, even as I write these words.

Scene 2: The Rapture of the Church

The next great picture Paul gives in 2 Thessalonians 2 is the Rapture of the Church:

> Do you not remember that when I was still with you I told you these things? And now you know what is restraining, that he may be revealed in his own time. For the mystery of lawlessness is already at work; only He who now restrains *will do so* until He is taken out of the way. And then the lawless one will be revealed, whom the Lord will consume with the breath of His mouth and destroy with the brightness of His coming (vv. 5–8).

Paul tells us something very important in that text. He says, "He who now restrains will do so until He is taken out of the way." So, who is the "He" that is restraining? The fact that the pronoun "He" is capitalized tells you that it is God Himself. More specifically, it is the Holy Spirit in the Church that is restraining sin and evil in the world today. And that will continue until the Rapture occurs and God's restraining force in the world will be removed.

Can you imagine a world with no Christians in it? Of course, that's difficult to imagine, but that is precisely how the world will be the very second the Rapture happens. In an instant so many things we may take for granted will disappear. There will be no more preaching about sin and repentance. Not a single person remaining will believe the Bible is the ultimate authority for faith and life. No one in the world will be leading others to Christ, except for the 144,000 Jews mentioned in Revelation chapters 7 and 14. It will be a completely transformed world—and not in a good way.

The Antichrist will not be revealed until after the Rapture occurs. People are always speculating about who the Antichrist is. Unfortunately, we live in a world with some great candidates for that role. I mean, if I were guessing, I could come up with my own top 10 list pretty quickly. But the truth is, I don't really know, and neither do you. It's not revealed yet. No one will know until after the Rapture, and I don't plan to be here.

In Luke 17, Jesus gives His own graphic description of the Rapture. He tells His followers what kind of world will exist before it happens. Jesus says, "As it was in the days of Noah, so it will be also in the days of the Son of Man" (v. 26). Jesus is saying, "Just like it was in the time of Noah, before the Great Flood, that's exactly how it will be before I return." He also says that people lived in the same way during Lot's time in the cities of Sodom and Gomorrah. Do you know what it was like during Noah and Lot's days and what will happen when Jesus returns? He tells us:

> They ate, they drank, they married wives, they were given in marriage, until the day that Noah entered the ark, and the flood came and destroyed them all. Likewise as it was also in the days of Lot: They ate, they drank, they bought, they sold, they planted, they built; but on the day that Lot went out of Sodom it rained fire and brimstone from heaven and destroyed *them* all. Even so will it be in the day when the Son of Man is revealed.

In that day, he who is on the housetop, and his goods *are* in the house, let him not come down to take them away. And likewise the one who is in the field, let him not turn back. Remember Lot's wife. Whoever seeks to save his life will lose it, and whoever loses his life will preserve it. I tell you, in that night there will be two *men* [or people] in one bed: the one will be taken and the other will be left. Two *women* will be grinding together: the one will be taken and the other left. Two *men* will be in the field: the one will be taken and the other left. The disciples asked Jesus, "Where, Lord?" He replied, "Wherever the body is, there the eagles will be gathered together" (Luke 17:27- 37).

The Rapture will be selective, and it is believers who will be selected. It doesn't matter if your wife or your husband is a Christian. It doesn't matter if your best friend is a Christian. It doesn't matter who you are related to or who your friends are. If you don't have a personal relationship with Jesus, then you won't be raptured. You will be left behind during the Tribulation and the reign of the most evil person in the history of the world.

Jesus said there will be buying and selling, marrying and giving in marriage before the Rapture, just as there was in the times of Noah and Lot. It will be business as usual. This is one of the reasons I believe so strongly that the Rapture will occur before the Tribulation. Let me point out a very important text from Luke chapter 17 that proves Jesus will return before the Tribulation.

Likewise as it was also in the days of Lot: They ate, they drank, they bought, they sold, they planted, they built; but **on the day that Lot**

went out of Sodom it rained fire and brimstone from heaven and destroyed *them* all. **Even so will it be in the day** when the Son of Man is revealed (Luke 17:28-30).

The angels that came to rescue Lot and his family told him that they could not judge Sodom and Gomorrah until Lot and his family were out and safely to their destination. (Genesis 19:22) And notice in the text from Luke 17 that Jesus said, "**On the day that Lot went out** of Sodom it rained fire and brimstone from heaven and destroyed them all. **Even so it will be in the day** the Son of Man is revealed" (emphasis added). Jesus is clearly talking about a specific day in Lot's life when he was taken out of harm's way before judgment fell. Jesus then directly links His return for His Church with that day and then graphically describes the Rapture. He couldn't have been more clear that it is a pre-wrath Rapture. Thank God!

People who insist that believers will go through the Tribulation ignore important texts like this that tell us clearly that Jesus will rapture us before judgment comes upon the earth. That is why Jesus described the days of Noah and Lot before the judgments came upon them—days of buying and selling, marrying and giving in marriage. At the end of the Tribulation, billions of people will have died, and the earth will be a smoldering ruin after seven years of horrific judgments from God. Nothing close to business as usual.

I have also heard Bible teachers who believe we will go through the Tribulation state that God will sovereignly shield believers from judgment and will protect His people just as He did for Israel in Goshen during the judgments God struck Egypt with through Moses. Again, those types of teachings ignore important Scripture texts such as these:

> And I saw thrones, and they sat on them, and judgment was committed to them. Then *I saw* the souls of those who had been beheaded for their witness to Jesus and for the word of God, who had not worshiped the beast or his image, and had not received *his* mark on their foreheads or on their hands. And they lived and reigned with Christ for a thousand years (Revelation 20:4).

> And he was given a mouth speaking great things and blasphemies, and he was given authority to continue for forty-two months. Then he opened his mouth in blasphemy against God, to blaspheme His name, His tabernacle, and those who dwell in heaven. It was granted to him to make war with the saints and to overcome them. And authority was given him over every tribe, tongue, and nation (Revelation 13:5–7).

The purpose of Bible prophecy is to comfort us. You cannot possibly comfort me by telling me that I will go through the Tribulation. It will be the most horrific seven years of human history. Not only will the Antichrist be persecuting and martyring believers in mass, but three plagues alone in Revelation chapter nine kill one-third of mankind. It will literally be hell on earth, and those who receive Christ after the Rapture will not be immune to any of it—except by God's mercy.

I am so thankful for the teachings of Jesus regarding the days of Noah and Lot. They give us great comfort that the Lord will not allow us to go through wrath but rather be miraculously rescued. I have been accused of being an escapist, and I openly admit that I am. And here is a Scripture from Jesus that tells all of us to be escapists:

> But take heed to yourselves, lest your hearts be weighed down with carousing, drunkenness, and cares of this life, and that Day come on you unexpectedly. For it will come as a snare on all those who dwell on the face of the whole earth. Watch therefore, and pray always that you may be counted worthy to escape all these things that will come to pass, and to stand before the Son of Man (Luke 21:34–36).

The setting of this passage from Jesus was His teaching the disciples about the end times and the judgments that would come upon the world during the Tribulation. In that context He directs us to pray that we will be able to "escape all these things that will come to pass, and to stand before the Son of Man." He is telling us to pray that we will rescued by Him in the Rapture and escape all of the judgments of the Tribulation. Yes, I'm an escapist, but I'm an obedient escapist!

THREE PARALLELS TO THE DAYS OF NOAH AND LOT

What did Jesus mean when He said the time before His coming will be like the days of Noah and Lot? I have discovered *three parallels* between the times of Noah and Lot and our present day.

1. An Immoral and Violent World

The Bible says the world was full of violence and immorality and in rebellion against God in the days of Noah. Lot's generation was known as an immoral generation. Consider the current world in which we live. Is it full of violence and immorality? Absolutely!

2. A Righteous Remnant

In the times of Noah and Lot, a righteous remnant who lived for God remained. Today, there are still many committed believers who are living for God in obedience to His Word.

3. The Sudden Removal of the Righteous

In 1 Thessalonians chapter 5, Paul writes about "the Day of the Lord." He tells the believers, "God did not appoint us to wrath" and instructs them to "comfort each other" (vv. 9, 11). In 1 Corinthians chapter 15, Paul gives us this vivid description of the Rapture:

Now this I say, brethren, that flesh and blood cannot inherit the kingdom of God; nor does corruption inherit incorruption. Behold, I tell you a mystery: We shall not all sleep, but we shall all be changed—in a moment, in the twinkling of an eye, at the last trumpet. For the trumpet will sound, and the dead will be raised incorruptible, and we shall be changed. For this corruptible must put on incorruption, and this mortal *must* put on immortality (1 Corinthians 15:50–53).

The Rapture will occur "in the twinkling of an eye". It is too little time to repent, change your life, make wrong things right, or give your life to Christ. This is why it is so important to understand end times prophecy and to be ready for the return of Jesus at any moment. This doesn't mean we have to be perfect people. None of us are perfect, and all of us are saved by grace, not by works.

But it is amazing to me in light of what the Bible says so clearly about the return of Jesus and the prophetic signs that are being fulfilled all around us that there are so many people living in sin and rebellion with little care about the future. They may look wise and cool right now, but in the twinkling of an eye, everything will change. And they will be left behind!

Scene Three: The Tribulation

In the third scene Paul describes the world once the Church is removed.

BELIEVE GOD AND HIS WORD,
AND THE TRIBULATION WILL
NOT BE YOUR DESTINY.

The coming of the *lawless one* is according to the working of Satan, with all power, signs, and lying wonders, and with all unrighteous deception among those who perish, because they did not receive the love of the truth, that they might be saved. And for this reason God will send them strong delusion, that they should believe the lie, that they all may be condemned who did not believe the truth but who had pleasure in unrighteousness (2 Thessalonians 2:9–12).

In Luke 17:32 Jesus tells His disciples to "remember Lot's wife." What do we remember about her? In Genesis 19 angels visited Lot's home in Sodom and strongly urged him to get his family out of the city. Still, Lot dawdled around, and the angels literally had to drag him and his family out of the city before the fire and brimstone fell. The angels told Lot and his family not to even look back. Lot's wife was fleeing along with him, but as the destruction began, she looked back and was turned into a pillar of salt. By using this story as a backdrop, Jesus is saying, "I'm coming back. This is the way the world is going to look before I return. And when I do, I'm going to leave one and take the other. So remember Lot's wife."

Jesus said, "But take heed to yourselves, lest your hearts be weighed down with carousing, drunkenness, and the cares of this life, and that Day come on you unexpectedly" (Luke 21:34). He is speaking of the Rapture in this verse. Then He says, "It will come as a snare on all those who dwell on the face of the whole earth" (v. 35). A snare is a trap laid for an animal. Jesus warns His followers to be ready when He comes and not to fall in love with the world, because that is what Lot's wife did. She loved her life in Sodom more than she loved God and more than she wanted to escape with her husband and daughters. Jesus' return will be like an animal trap for every person who loves the world more than they love Him. And "every person" means it will be a global event. How should Jesus' followers respond? He tells them, "Watch therefore and pray always that you may be counted worthy to escape all these things that will come to pass and to stand before the Son of Man" (v. 36).

For those who are left behind, the lawless one—the Antichrist—is going to come with signs, wonders, power, and lies. He will pour out his unrighteous deception on everyone on earth, and they will believe it to their own destruction. If they would have received the love of the Father and the truth of His Son, they would have been saved, but they will give into lies instead. They will give themselves over to delusion, and the Antichrist will be the king of delusions.

As I said before, this is not a message of despair. It is a message of hope and grace. Believe God and His Word, and the Tribulation will not be your destiny. Ask yourself this question: *what is my relationship with the Bible?* Compare it to a romantic relationship. Are you dating the Bible? Are you engaged to it? Or are you married to God's Word? These are some of the most important questions you can ask yourself today. Spend five minutes on the internet, and you will realize Christians are being attacked every day because they believe the Bible's teaching on truth and morality. When you see such things, do you duck behind the corner, afraid you will reveal what you really believe? Do you know what Jesus said about crouching in fear?

> For whoever is ashamed of Me and My words in this adulterous and sinful generation, of him the Son of Man also will be ashamed when He comes in the glory of His Father with the holy angels (Mark 8:38).

We are living in a world that is launching a full-fledged attack on Jesus Christ, His Word, and everything else that is holy and sacred. That fact can discourage you, or you can be assured that we are the people who are living on this earth just prior to the return of Jesus. Do you want to be like the wise virgins in Jesus' parable? Then don't be a person who is ashamed of Jesus and His Word. Yes, you should show compassion towards unbelievers and avoid self-righteousness, but don't be ashamed. Your King is coming!

When you recognize a person who is not yet a believer—and I say "not yet" because I hope they soon will be—or you see someone who is not living in obedience before God, show compassion. Christians should be gracious people. Nevertheless, don't compromise the truth of God's Word for anyone. Jesus was full of grace and truth—*both of them* (John 1:14). He expects the same from us. If you have truth without grace, then you are performing spiritual surgery without anesthesia. On the other hand, if you are full of grace but neglect the truth, then you are dispensing a medicine bottle with no medicine in it to cure anyone. Only grace and truth *together* can bring about anyone's healing.

Don't be so gracious that you're willing to give up the truth of the Bible just to make people feel better about themselves. Remember, the person who loves you the most isn't the one who tells you what you want to hear. The one who really loves you will tell you what you *need* to hear. Did Jesus cause offenses? Of course, He did. But it was because He was the only person with the truth. And His truth was loving and full of grace. I urge you to be like Jesus, both gracious and truthful. As you observe people who aren't living for God—people who are in bondage or even people who are rejecting the Word of God—then by the power of the Holy Spirit, love them. Show compassion. But in the process, hold on tight to the Word of God. I am unwilling to give up the truth of the Bible for anyone. The truth of the Bible saved my life, and by God's grace I will uphold it until He returns.

MORALITY AT A
TIPPING POINT

6

WHEN MORALITY IS OPTIONAL

If you haven't already noticed, the world is at a moral tipping point. I believe we are living in the most immoral time in human history. Our lives and the lives of our children have been morally upended by the debauchery available to us through advanced communications technology now accessible around the globe. Homes all over the world contain cell phones, electronic tablets, computers, and satellite televisions that were not available to previous generations. Every thinkable and unthinkable form of immorality is available in an instant almost everywhere on the planet.

A few years ago I was preaching in another American city. The church's pastor and I were having a discussion before it was time for me to preach. Then he shocked me with this news: "Jimmy, I'm going to have to call an emergency meeting of the parents of our church. I have to talk to them and inform them about a new level of immorality in our city's high schools." I was curious about what he would tell them, so I replied, "Really? What is going on?" His church is in a major city, so I could only guess where he was going with this information. "Jimmy," he said, "My son goes to a public high school. I have learned from him that there is a new term, and it's not 'homosexuality' or 'bisexuality.' No, the new term is 'pansexuality.'" This may not be news to you, as it has been a few years since I preached in that church, but I had not encountered this term before. The prefix *pan-* means "all." This pastor was telling me that in his son's high school there were students who no longer limited their sexuality by any specific definition. In this city's schools and now all over the planet, there are people who will have sex with anyone or anything as long as they feel like it. There are no limits. It doesn't even require another person. I'm not going to go any further with this definition. The reality is worse than your imagination.

Humans have included sexual immorality in their repertoire since the beginning of history; the Bible records it. Even so, we are seeing the erosion of sexual morality happening at a blistering pace. I will discuss the erosion of sexual morality more in the next chapter, but I want you to see it is part of a bigger picture. It's unlike anything humanity has ever seen before. I know another pastor whose best friend has a son. That son became suicidal. The pastor told me, "This boy is involved in pornography, and he's addicted to it." He then told me that the son was not even looking at real people. He was in love with fantasy characters and realized he would never be able to fulfill his fantasies. I will spare you any more details. But isn't that the way the devil operates? Our enemy wants to addict us to something we can't possibly fulfill.

God does not act in that way. There is nothing about God that is addictive. No one has ever been addicted to reading the Bible. No one has ever gotten addicted to prayer. No one will ever be addicted to worship. God does not imprison us the way addiction does. He wants your sincere, willing worship—not your enslavement. He's a Shepherd, not a slave driver. The devil, however, does want to be your slave driver. He wants you to fall into addiction, because then he can control you and keep you from reaching God's destiny for your life. I am telling you our current world is in a moral free-fall, with all sorts of addictions to all types of sinful behaviors. According to the Bible, it is yet another sign of the end times.

In the previous chapter I talked at length about three parallels between the days of Noah and Lot that Jesus spoke about in Luke chapter 17 and the days in which we are living. But there is actually a fourth parallel that is important to remember.

CATACLYSMIC JUDGMENT

The fourth parallel is cataclysmic judgment. I do not mean a run-of-the-mill tragedy. This judgment is *the wrath of God* poured out. In the time of Noah, a flood came upon the world and destroyed every living person, except for Noah and his family. This was not simply a bad day, a bad war, a rumor of a war, an earthquake, or a pestilence such as COVID-19. This event was overwhelming global destruction. In the cities of Sodom and Gomorrah, fire and brimstone fell in the shape of hail. It rained down from heaven and destroyed every human, except Lot and his family. The Tribulation will be worse than anything the world has ever seen.

Once again, I return to the book of 1 Thessalonians, where Paul discusses the return of Christ. Here the apostle tells believers they will not experience God's wrath (5:9). The Tribulation is much more than judgment—it is the wrath of Almighty God poured out on the whole earth. Also, the apostle John writes in Revelation that one third of humanity will be destroyed (9:15) by three plagues. For that reason, at the end of the Tribulation, there will be no buying or selling, nor will there be marrying and giving in marriage. The world's economies will collapse, and billions will die. The earth will be a smoldering ruin. There will be no more business as usual.

Paul also writes:

> They themselves declare concerning us what manner of entry we had to you, and how you turned to God from idols to serve the living and true God, and to wait for His Son from heaven, whom He raised from the dead, *even* Jesus **who delivers us from the wrath to come** (1 Thessalonians 1:9–10, emphasis added).

Jesus will deliver believers from the wrath that is to come. Paul repeats this idea a few chapters later:

> God did not appoint us to wrath, but to obtain salvation through our Lord Jesus Christ, who died for us, that whether we wake

or sleep, we should live together with Him. Therefore comfort each other and edify one another, just as you also are doing (1 Thessalonians 5:9–11).

Why is it so important to me that you know you won't see the horror of the Tribulation? I have the same motivation Paul had. I want to comfort you. I want you to know God is overflowing with grace and mercy. His love for you knows no end. Believers, we will not experience the Tribulation because our God has not appointed us to wrath. He will not judge us along with the world. We are already part of His new creation, not the old one. He will come to rescue us in the Rapture, just as He delivered Noah and Lot. We will not go through seven years of hell on earth, where billions will die and those who live will endure unspeakable torment. No, you and I will be marrying Jesus in heaven. We have nothing to fear!

Take another look at Noah's world:

This is the genealogy of Noah. Noah was a just man, perfect in his generations. Noah walked with God. And Noah begot three sons: Shem, Ham, and Japheth. The earth was also corrupt before God, and the earth was filled with violence. So God looked upon the earth, and indeed it was corrupt; for all flesh had corrupted their way on the earth. And God said to Noah, "The end of all flesh has come before Me, for the earth is filled with violence through them; and behold, I will destroy them with the earth" (Genesis 6:9–13).

The word translated "corrupt" in this chapter is *shachath* in Hebrew. It means 'evil, filthy, and immoral.' Can you see the parallels to our present world? God surveyed the world of Noah, and what He saw was not merely a bad world; it was an *evil* world. Noah and his family lived in a violent and immoral society, much like the one we are living in today.

Now take another look at Lot's world:

> For if God did not spare the angels who sinned, but cast *them* down to hell and delivered *them* into chains of darkness, to be reserved for judgment; and did not spare the ancient world, but saved Noah, *one* of *eight* people, a preacher of righteousness, bringing in the flood on the world of the ungodly; and turning the cities of Sodom and Gomorrah into ashes, condemning *them* to destruction, making *them* an example to those who afterward would live ungodly; and delivered righteous Lot, *who was* oppressed by the filthy conduct of the wicked (for that righteous man, dwelling among them, tormented *his* righteous soul from day to day by seeing and hearing their lawless deeds)—*then* the Lord knows how to deliver the godly out of temptations and to reserve the unjust under punishment for the day of judgment, and especially those who walk according to the flesh in the lust of uncleanness and despise authority. *They are* presumptuous and self-willed. They are not afraid to speak evil of dignitaries, whereas angels, who are greater in power and might, do not bring a reviling accusation against them before the Lord (2 Peter 2:4–11).

The apostle Peter uses the word *aselgeia* in this passage, which is translated "filthy." It means 'shameless, immoral, and full of wrong desires.' According to Peter, people who are "filthy" have overwhelming desires for pleasure and absolutely no fear of

God. The angels came into the city to deliver Lot and his family, and the men of the city tried to force themselves sexually on the angels. I don't know if you can get any more ungodly. When God looked upon those cities in the days of Lot, it appeared to Him very much like our world does today. He answered their immorality in a very severe way through cataclysmic judgment, which will also come upon our world soon. When God saw Noah's immoral and violent world, He had the same response. God will have to apologize to Noah and Lot if He allows our world to continue as it is.

THE BIBLE ASSESSES THE MORAL STATE OF OUR WORLD

The apostle Paul delineates a much more descriptive assessment of our world. He tells Timothy about the state of morality in the last days:

> But know this, that in the last days perilous times will come: For men will be lovers of themselves, lovers of money, boasters, proud, blasphemers, disobedient to parents, unthankful, unholy, unloving, unforgiving, slanderers, without self-control, brutal, despisers of good, traitors, headstrong, haughty, lovers of pleasure rather than lovers of God, having a form of godliness but denying its power. And from such people turn away! For of this sort are those who creep into households and make captives of gullible women loaded down with sins, led away by various lusts, and always learning and never able to come to the knowledge of the truth. Now as Jannes

and Jambres resisted Moses, so do these also resist the truth: men of corrupt minds, disapproved concerning the faith but they will progress no further, for their folly will be manifest to all, as theirs also was (2 Timothy 3:1–9).

Would you agree that Paul's description seems very much like our present day? He lists 19 separate moral violations and says there will be a wholesale deconstruction of morality in the world. I do not believe this was the state of the world when I was a child. When I misbehaved at school, my parents didn't complain or call the ACLU. They never threatened any of my teachers. No, if my parents discovered I had caused trouble at school, I had big trouble on my hands at home. We left our doors unlocked. We played outside day and night, and neither we nor our parents had any fear about it. Today, parents would be considered highly irresponsible if they did the same thing, because of the evil people who roam our neighborhoods. Yes, there were immoral people back then, but most people were generally moral. It was a very different world.

Why Paul Describes Immorality in 19 Different Ways

Today we are witnessing a complete rejection of morality, especially since the advent of the internet. In the past quarter century, we have watched the world around us change. So, when Paul uses 19 different measures of immorality as signals for the end times, his second letter to Timothy looks more up-to-date today than it did even 25 years ago. The apostle tells Timothy some very dangerous times are coming in the end, and he then goes into great detail to describe them. But why do you suppose Paul lists all 19 moral violations?

1. TO EXPLAIN THE FULL SPECTRUM OF SIN

Paul is explaining the full spectrum of sin that will be in the world in the end times. Immorality isn't simply about sexuality, although it includes that aspect of our lives. Immorality is really a measure of character. If people fall into gross immorality, then it affects every fiber of their character. In the same way that cancer begins with a single cell and can eventually overtake the body, people who choose immorality soon have a complete takeover of their character and existence. Morals are there to protect you, others, and your relationship with God.

Suppose I am a moral person. (I think I am, but I want to be humble about it.) If so, then I'm not going to hurt you intentionally. I won't lash out and say something terrible to or about you. I wouldn't tell a lie about you or to you. I would never malign your character. I wouldn't steal from you or damage something that belongs to you. I would never try to seduce your wife. If I am a moral person, then it is safe for you and the people you love to be around me. On the other hand, if I'm an immoral person, then I will end up damaging you in one or more ways. You cannot be safe around immorality.

2. TO EXPRESS GOD'S FEELINGS ABOUT IMMORALITY

Paul wants Timothy to understand that God hates immorality and will judge it severely. When the apostle says, "Lovers of themselves, lovers of money, boasters, proud," all of these things are truly "unloving." The Greek word translated in English as "unloving" is *astorgos*, which means 'without a natural family love for each other.' When I began in ministry over four decades ago, a woman would rarely leave her family, especially not her children. Some men did not behave so well, and some of them would abandon their wives and children. But for a woman to do that would be very rare. At present, I have witnessed parents of both genders abandon their children, abuse them, or even prey upon them. We have reached a disturbing era in which many parents have no natural regard for their very own offspring. Some will even go as far as to kill them.

Sadly, I have witnessed the results firsthand and in a very personal way. Just a few years ago, I conducted a funeral for a couple who died as the result of a murder-suicide. You see, I knew them very well. I grew up with them and went to elementary school with them. In this case the woman killed her husband and then herself.

Another one of my longtime friends, a man who was instrumental in my accepting Jesus and growing in my faith, moved to another city. He stopped going to church and began hanging around with a very ungodly man. I spoke with my friend about his choices several times. I asked him why he had dropped out of church and why he was hanging out with a notoriously immoral man. He responded, "Well, I'm just in a different phase of my life. I really don't need church right now, and I'm evangelizing this man." Some days later, I received a call from his wife. I could hear their children screaming in the background. Her voice began to quiver, and she said, "He's leaving me, right now, and moving to live with his friend." I was shocked and angry. I replied, "What do you mean he's leaving you? Put him on the phone." So she handed the phone to her husband, and I asked him, "Are you actually leaving your wife?" He responded, "Yes. I'm going to live with my friend there, Jimmy. You can't imagine all the sex that's out there. And I'm getting away from my family so I can go out and have fun, have sex, and live my life."

This man didn't leave his family for a woman; he left his family for *women!* Before he could hang up, I urged, "You stay right there. I'm on my way. I'll be there in just a minute." He said, "No, no. I'm … I'm not … I'm on my way out." Before he left, he told his wife, "You're the perfect wife. You just don't give me enough sex." Please pay close attention. *If you're under the influence of pornography, a harem of women can't give you enough sex.* You have a perverted sense of reality. This man was indeed under pornography's sway. Then he had the nerve to ask me to go with him. I won't tell you exactly how I responded, but I can assure you it wasn't my kindest moment.

Beyond that, I want you to know what else happened during that call. I could hear his children pleading in the background, "Daddy, don't leave! Daddy, please don't leave! Daddy! Daddy!" Three children cried in the most pitiful chorus you could ever hear. Their heart-wrenching screams have stuck with me all these years. His wife later told me they were on his legs, clutching them with all of their strength. Finally, he pried them loose when he reached the front door. And then he was gone, off to get his "needs" met. This man destroyed his wife, his children, and his whole family. He demolished his reputation. Even worse, he threw away his relationship with the God who loves him so much. He only cared about himself and what he could get. That is the world we live in today.

God hates immorality because it destroys the people He loves. It leaves damage in its wake as it devastates men, women, and children. Our God is loving and does not wish evil to come upon us. He created morality to protect the people He loves. Immorality devastates and ruins. That's why Paul told Timothy, "Beware in the last days—dangerous times are going to come." Believers, we are in dangerous times right now. We live is an age with no moral restraints. You will hear of enraged employees who come back to the factory or office and shoot people. It's a spiritually and physically very, very dangerous world. We live in a time of perverted values, misplaced loyalties, and thoughtless acts.

MORALS ARE THERE TO
PROTECT YOU, OTHERS, AND
YOUR RELATIONSHIP WITH GOD.

Four Categories of Immorality

The 19 specific moral issues Paul lists can be divided into four general categories:

1. EXALTATION OF SELF

The first category of immorality Paul addresses is the exaltation of self, which we might also call narcissism in contemporary terms. He says people will be lovers of self, boasters, proud, haughty, and headstrong. Most of us have seen athletes who may be a bit boastful or seem to be a little full of themselves. I think some of that is fine. It's almost become part of the game. When I was a boy, though, no one did that kind of bragging in professional sports. A player would do something great, but there wouldn't be any excessive celebrating. When I would watch my beloved Dallas Cowboys, Bob Lilly or Roger Staubach would make an awesome play. Then they would walk back to the huddle like they had just gone outside to get the mail from the mailbox. Coaches told players, "Act like you've been there before." Fans celebrated, of course, but not the players. Back then, it was considered wrong to celebrate your own accomplishments.

Then the times began to change. The first time I saw an athlete celebrate his own success, it was during a Dallas Cowboy game. The player actually did a backflip after he made a great play. Cowboy's coach Tom Landry pulled him out of the game. He was not going to let his players act that way. Today, however, it looks as though players have hired professional choreographers to help them plan their celebrations. Again, I don't want to be overly critical; I recognize it has become socially acceptable to do some celebration. But that is because society changed. This shift in behavior exemplifies a general self-centeredness that has invaded our culture.

How many people dream of being celebrities, even if they are only famous on the internet? How often do we hear about the ostentatious lifestyles of people who have no more talent than you or me? We are living in a world full of socially-sanctioned narcissism. Nothing matters except me or what other people can do for me. The problem isn't that people love themselves; rather, it is that they love themselves to the exclusion of God and everyone else.

2. REJECTION OF AUTHORITY

The apostle Paul says many people will reject authority in the last days. They will be "disobedient to parents" and "lovers of pleasure rather than lovers of God." I have some dire news if you are in authority: this is a dangerous world for you. Law enforcement personnel in the US are under assault, as they are elsewhere around the world. These individuals guard our society for low-level wages, yet they have become prime targets for both physical and legal assaults. In Dallas, Texas, our own police force has been attacked many times with deadly force.

Teachers also face a society that no longer respects their role. One teacher I know told me a boy in his class said to him, "I'm going to go home and get my gun and come back and kill you." The teacher expelled the student. At the end of the day, the teacher was walking to his car when he encountered the student's mother. She said to him, "If you wouldn't make my son mad, then he wouldn't threaten you with his gun."

My parents would not have been so gracious to me, and they certainly wouldn't have confronted my teacher. Sadly, the student probably threatened his mother in the same way whenever he became angry with her. Teachers need authority to teach. However, we are moving toward an increasingly lawless society in which no one fears or respects authority. Remember, the Antichrist will be called "the lawless one." When you are in rebellion against authority, you have the same spirit as the Antichrist.

3. REJECTION OF MORAL STANDARDS

A few years ago the members of a very famous boy band attended our church. Before I stood to preach, one of our pastors said to me, "If you hear girls screaming, it's not about you." Just for clarification, there is no time in my life I would have thought that it was about me. Anyway, each of the boys had committed to chastity, and they made agreements with God to wait until marriage before they had sex. They were treated as an oddity by some and vilified by the press. They were openly mocked. However, I believe we need many more young people to commit to purity before marriage. How many times have we heard, "It's my body, and you can't tell me what to do with it"? But when people like these boys decide they will use their bodies for good rather than sin, they are ridiculed for doing so. Paul warned there would be despisers of good, and he was definitely right.

4. VICIOUS AND UNLOVING

Paul says people in the last days will also be disloyal, unloving, and verbally vicious. They will be unforgiving and unwilling to reconcile. They will be blasphemers, slanderers, and traitors. In my experience, this seems to be a lot of what I am seeing on the internet. In fact, some children have even committed suicide because of what has been said to and about them on blogs and other social media sites. We live in a culture with an entire media industry dedicated to gossip, and they don't care whose lives they destroy. They will pounce on any opportunity to pour out their poison.

President Franklin D. Roosevelt was a polio survivor, and it left him wheelchair-bound most of his adult life. Do you realize most Americans were not aware of his condition until long after his death? Do you know why? The media protected his image. They didn't want the American people to see their president as weak. Whenever Roosevelt took the stage, he was helped to stand behind a podium, or the photographers took shots of him that made him look standing and strong. Today, however, it seems to be one of the top goals of the media to disgrace and embarrass anyone and everyone they dislike.

Four Moral Responses for Believers

The world we live in today is nothing like the one many of us encountered in our youth. We are witnessing all four categories of immorality that Paul lists for Timothy. This is a world in the end times. I will say it again: we are at a tipping point. What if, however, believers want to live counter to the spiritual decline of our age? What would that look like? Suppose I were to reverse Paul's list and show you the life of a godly person. What would be the moral opposites of Paul's four categories?

1. EXALTATION OF CHRIST OVER SELF

Godly people should be neither haughty nor proud. Rather, they are humble and exalt Christ over themselves. The apostle Peter says, "Be clothed with humility" (1 Peter 5:5). Why do you suppose he says we must "clothe" ourselves? It is because we don't put humility on naturally. We have to make a choice to do it. Because of our sin nature, we are prideful. We have to make a choice to allow God to do a work in us so we will put aside our old prideful selves.

Every day you have to get out of your bed and make the decision to put on humility and walk in it the rest of the day. Once you become a follower of Christ, your life isn't about you anymore; it's about Jesus. When you realize this truth, you will spend much less time trying to make sure others think well of you. Your first thought will be, *I need Jesus, so I am going to praise and worship Him as my first act of the day.* It won't be, *How do I promote myself?* No, it will be, *How can I glorify Jesus and lift Him up so that others will see Him?* I will only be visible in the background.

While reading the book of Revelation one day, I saw these words: "A great multitude which no one could number" (7:9). These people were gathered to worship God. Then I read about "a sea of glass mingled with fire," on which people were again worshipping God (15:2–3). Do you know what went through my mind as I was reading these Scriptures? *It isn't about me! It will never be about me. It's about Jesus. Get over yourself, Jimmy!* Yes, there will be a lot of interesting things to see and do in heaven. And if I'm honest, a glass and fire sea sounds really interesting! But heaven won't be about me. Only one Person is worthy of my eternal attention and worship—the Lord Jesus Christ. As believers, we must take off our arrogant, narcissistic clothing, put on humility, and exalt Jesus.

2. SUBMISSION TO GOD'S AUTHORITY AND HIS DELEGATED HUMAN AUTHORITIES

As a Christian, I am supposed to be a submitted person. You see, when I claimed Jesus as Lord, I agreed with Him that I had been out of control and needed to be under His control. Because I am a Christian, a *follower* of Christ, I am not destined to be a rebel. Rebellion is neither congruous nor compatible with the Christian faith. I must be submitted to God's authority and also to the human authorities He has delegated. Remember, Jesus said, "I do nothing unless I see My Father doing it" (see John 5:19–20). Jesus also submitted to His mother, Mary, who was God's designated authority in His life. Mary prevented Jesus from entering into public ministry when He was 13 years old (see Luke 2:41–52). When Jesus was 30, his mother was the one who told Him to begin His public ministry (John 2:1–11). Jesus submitted to authority, both in heaven and on earth.

3. ACCEPTANCE OF THE BIBLE'S MORAL STANDARDS

The third way to counter the immoral spirit of this age is by accepting and living by the Bible's absolute moral standards. Our fleshly selves want to do things the Bible expressly says we should not do. Or we don't do the things the Bible specifically tells us to do. I understand that we all fail and make mistakes. However, there's a huge distinction between committing a sin and actively choosing to practice a sinful lifestyle. Yes, Christians sin, but someone who really loves Jesus won't say, *God, everything You tell me to do, I reject. Everything I once believed, I now renounce. I am going to handle life on my own from now on.*

If I choose to practice sin, it means I am saying, "I'm doing it. It's okay. I'll do anything I want to do any time I want to do it. Then I'll find a Scripture to make it look right. It's my lifestyle. It's just the way I live." The apostle Paul says, "If you confess with your mouth the Lord Jesus and believe in your heart that God raised Him from the dead, you will be saved" (Romans 10:9).

And Jesus asked, "Why do you call me 'Lord, Lord,' and not do the things which I say?" (Luke 6:46). We must understand that Lord means "Master." A master has authority over how servants behave. Is Jesus the Master over your life or not?

God isn't a vending machine from which you can take what you want and leave everything else. You can't say, "I'm going to push C-7 and get a Savior, but Lord, you stay put." Jesus won't come to you on your terms. It's His way or no way. Some people think they can tell Him, "Lord, I want to be saved, and I want you to be the Lord of my life. But let me tell You something. I'm going to sleep with anyone I want. I have a list of things You can't talk to me about, so I'm just going to put that out there, Jesus." I can imagine the Lord saying, "Really? So you think you are in control of this relationship? Really?"

To counter the spirit of this age, you must accept, believe, rely on, and live according to the absolute, infallible, and inspired Word of Almighty God. The Bible will tell you the truth whenever everything and everyone else around you is telling a lie. If you wonder if something is a sin, you can be sure the Holy Spirit's voice and the Word of God will give you a clear answer.

4. LOVING OTHERS LOYALLY AND SACRIFICIALLY

Remember, Paul says in the end times people will be unloving, refuse to reconcile or forgive, and be blasphemers. Jesus gives an alternative way for us to behave:

ONLY ONE PERSON IS WORTHY
OF MY ETERNAL ATTENTION
AND WORSHIP—THE LORD
JESUS CHRIST.

Blessed *are* the peacemakers,
For they shall be called sons of God (Matthew 5:9).

Believers shouldn't be troublemakers, gossips, or mean-spirited people. Jesus is telling us to love others loyally and sacrificially. I believe it was under these conditions that America became a great nation. Our founding fathers and mothers had this character. This spirit governed our nation while we were ascending in greatness. Today, however, we have become a very immoral and vicious nation. We have condoned abortion, sexual immorality, violence, and every other category by which you would judge a nation to have fallen into immorality. We have come very close to renouncing the exceptional calling God has on us and the blessing He has placed on America.

Jesus told His followers:

You are the salt of the earth; but if the salt loses its flavor, how shall it be seasoned? It is then good for nothing but to be thrown out and trampled underfoot by men. You are the light of the world. A city that is set on a hill cannot be hidden. Nor do they light a lamp and put it under a basket, but on a lampstand, and it gives light to all *who are* in the house. Let your light so shine before men, that they may see your good works and glorify your Father in heaven (Matthew 5:13–16).

Is this the way you think most people are living? Even most Christians? In these last days it is more important than ever for us to be a light to the world. Our lives must show people the way to God. Rather than us being under the world's influence, we should influence the world. People may try to draw you into sin, but your job is to draw other people into righteousness and a relationship with Jesus Christ. God intends for us to have an aggressive offense rather than a passive defense. He wants us to live our lives intentionally with the purpose of glorifying God, preparing for Jesus' return, and taking as many people to heaven along with us as we possibly can.

We cannot reduce all immorality to sexual immorality, although people in the world often accuse Christians of taking that approach. We are often portrayed as no-fun, judgmental Pharisees. To the contrary, Bible-believing Christians should know just how much God wants us to enjoy our sexuality within healthy marriages. The Bible also tells us just how destructive other forms of sexual expression can be. In fact, you don't have to read the Bible to see the devastation caused by sex outside of the boundaries of the biblical definition of marriage. Since sex without limits causes such incredible harm to our society, I will devote the next chapter to demonstrating how unchecked sexuality fits into the Bible's prophecies of the end times.

7

SEXUALITY IN REBELLION

All immorality is sin against God, but sexual immorality is given specific attention in the New Testament. Jesus said that the end times would be very much like the days of Noah and Lot (Luke 17:26–30). In both biblical stories sexual immorality pervaded the society. I believe these are the only two times in human history when sexual morality reached such a severe decline. In both cases the culture devolved to the point of moral anarchy, and God answered with cataclysmic judgment.

The apostle Peter said God did not even spare sexually immoral angels from His wrath (2 Peter 2:4–10). Verse 10 of that passage presents two defining features of the type of society Jesus was talking about in Luke 17. Peter addresses "those who indulge in the lust of defiling passion and despise authority." What he is referring to is *sexual immorality* and *rebellion*. That is the perfect description of our society today. And what will be the result of our ungodly behaviors? God will unleash His judgment, and the fullest judgment will be the Tribulation. I will show you the kinds of behaviors I am writing about.

SEXUAL IMMORALITY

Humans have been sinners since Adam and Eve disobeyed God in the Garden of Eden, but during specific periods immorality has been so rampant that God intervened with catastrophic results. Right now, we have invented things in our time that would shock the generations of Noah and Lot. I will not go into every detail, but I want to tell you about *four innovations* in our time that have compromised sexual morality beyond what any previous generation could imagine.

1. Global Distribution of Explicit Pornography

Anyone who has access to a phone, computer, or other digital device today can access the most explicit pornography humanity has ever invented. Only a few years ago, people had to sneak off to a convenience store or pornography shop to purchase pornographic materials. Generally, this purchase was done in secret with the threat of exposure and shame. Today, however, millions of Americans and others around the world view explicit and even violent pornographic materials from the comfort and privacy of their own homes, offices, and even vehicles.

One attempt to produce a study on the effects of pornography usage among college-aged young men failed to materialize when researchers could not identify a control group who did not view pornography. Another study found that four separate one-hour long exposures to R-rated materials modified men's perceptions of women enough to influence how they would relate to them sexually. Imagine the effects that constant exposure to graphic pornographic materials has on the minds and behaviors of those who consume it. Pornography has negative effects on relationships and has destroyed untold millions of marriages.

2. Virtual and Robotic Sex

Pornography has become a private affair with an increasingly limited risk of exposure. This supposed privacy only feeds our society's obsession with self-focused and selfish sexual expression. God created sexuality to be servant-oriented with a concern for others, specifically oriented toward a spouse in a marital relationship. The sacredness of sexuality has been decontextualized from the marriage relationship. As sexuality intersects with modern technology, humans have become even more inventive with self-focused sexual expression. Ever newer inventions in virtual reality and robotics vie to replace human interactions entirely. Every year, inventors reveal new types of technology to replace humans in the sexual equation. Some people have become so obsessed with this new technology that they even claim they are in love with their sex robots in the same way we would describe a romantic relationship with another human.

3. Pansexuality

I discussed pansexuality in the previous chapter, but to reiterate, it is the idea that a person can be open to sexual experiences with a person of either gender or with someone who does not identify with a gender. This is a relatively new phenomenon and considered "cool" or "avant-garde" by many people in the younger generations. It is an expression of sexual rebellion and a refusal to follow social or religious morals or norms. For example, pop star Miley Cyrus has identified herself as pansexual and publicly engages in relationships with both males and females.

4. Transsexuality

Transsexuality has been openly practiced since at least the 1960s. Recently, it has become mainstream. Caitlyn (formerly Bruce) Jenner was once the most celebrated Olympic athlete in the world. In 2015 Jenner announced he would be transitioning from male to female. Many celebrities and politicians celebrated his "courage." ESPN announced Jenner as the recipient of that year's *Arthur Ashe Courage Award*. Some athletes and sports commentators expressed their dismay at the award but were soon met with public disapproval and scorn.

Transsexuality is often referred to as "gender reassignment." The thought behind making these reassignments is that humans are simply biological accidents, and gender is socially constructed. If a person feels he or she has been given the wrong gender assignment, medical procedures can correct the error. To hold this position a person must believe either that there is no God, or He exists but is a bungling idiot, much the same way an absent-minded scientist would create a disaster by mixing the wrong chemicals. The Bible, however, presents God in a different light. The psalmist writes:

> For You formed my inward parts;
> You covered me in my mother's womb.
> I will praise You, for I am fearfully *and* wonderfully made;
> Marvelous are Your works,
> And *that* my soul knows very well.
> My frame was not hidden from You,
> When I was made in secret,
> *And* skillfully wrought in the lowest parts of the earth.
> Your eyes saw my substance, being yet unformed.
> And in Your book they all were written,
> The days fashioned for me,
> When *as yet there were* none of them.
> How precious also are Your thoughts to me, O God!
> How great is the sum of them!
> *If* I should count them, they would be more in number than the sand;
> When I awake, I am still with You (Psalm 139:13–18).

If we are fearfully and wonderfully made by God, and He doesn't make mistakes, then why would people assume they have been assigned the wrong gender? I understand there are some people who struggle in this area, and they need a compassionate response, but I will not accept that the answer rests in mutilating yourself.

The idea of transsexuality as an option for sexual expression is the result of demonic lies that have been implanted through trauma, rejection, sin, or other open doors meant to confuse and distort human sexuality. The fact is that you cannot change or reassign your gender. The closest modern science can get is to offer mere cosmetic changes. A well-known sex change surgeon admitted that removing male genitalia does not result in reassigning a person from male to female. The best it can do is neuter an otherwise healthy male. Any gender change is in name only. A change can be made, to be sure, but the truth is no female parts replace those that are male or vice versa. Even sadder, 41 percent of participants who undergo surgical changes subsequently attempt suicide.[53] They are disappointed because the true change they thought they had received never materializes. Instead of feeling sexually different, they realize they have now actually become sexually dead. No amount of surgery or hormones can correct that feeling.

Again, Christians must respond with true compassion. The devil is attacking people with these feelings of gender confusion. They don't know where to turn or what to do. Even so, as believers, we must stand firm on God's Word (Mark 8:38). God has given us the assignment to lead people to the truth and to take authority over the devil and his lies (Luke 10:19).

THE BIBLICAL VIEW OF SEXUALITY

The best way to combat the devil's deception is with the truth of God's Word. Before the fall of humanity as the result of sin, sexuality was beautiful. Genesis says, "And they were both naked, the man and his wife, and were not ashamed" (Genesis 2:25). After the fall, however, the picture dramatically changed. Instead of beauty, sexuality became confused and perverted. Genesis gives this account:

> And they heard the sound of the LORD God walking in the garden in the cool of the day, and Adam and his wife hid themselves from the presence of the LORD God among the trees of the garden.
> Then the LORD God called to Adam and said to him, "Where *are* you?"
> So he said, "I heard Your voice in the garden, and I was afraid because I was naked; and I hid myself."
> And He said, "Who told you that you *were* naked? Have you eaten from the tree of which I commanded you that you should not eat?" (Genesis 3:8–11).

They only knew they were naked after they listened to Satan's voice. He operates by stealth, which makes him both dangerous and effective. Satan focuses his attacks on our sexuality, as he did with Adam and Eve, because he knows it determines our futures and that of our society and many generations to come.

God is calling all people, but particularly Christians, to return to a biblical view of sexuality. What then are the elements of this biblical view?

1. Marriage as a Covenant Relationship

The Bible views sexuality within the bounds of a covenantal marriage relationship between a man and a woman. The Hebrew word from which the word covenant derives literally means 'to cut.' In the Genesis account, God physically cut Adam and removed a rib to create Eve (Genesis 2:22). God's act created a permanent physical bond between Adam and his wife. Similarly, the marital covenant between a man and a woman is a permanent, sacrificial relationship of blessing. It is neither casual nor temporary. It is not self-centered or even self-actualizing. Rather, two people join with each other and build their lives around this covenant. For them to do this safely and securely, the bond must be permanent. The marital covenant exceeds a mere contract and permanently changes the identity of both the man and the woman.

2. Sex Within the Covenant Relationship

Since God intends marriage to be a special type of relationship, He offers sex between a husband and wife as the sacred covenant seal and sign of their marriage. Sex consummates or formalizes the marriage union. I would say it this way: it seals the deal. All valid covenants have a seal and a sign. Sex between a husband and wife seals the covenant, while the sign of the marital covenant is the ongoing good faith of the couple as they meet their spouse's sexual needs energetically and with a good attitude.

THE MARITAL COVENANT
BETWEEN A MAN AND A WOMAN
IS A PERMANENT, SACRIFICIAL
RELATIONSHIP OF BLESSING.

For example, circumcision became the seal and sign of Abraham's covenant with God. Similarly, Christians submit to baptism as a seal of their covenant with Jesus Christ, and communion (the Lord's Supper) reconfirms the covenant as an ongoing sign of good faith. The seals and signs of covenants are important and powerful acts of obedience and relationship. God powerfully blesses them when we honor them. Abraham's circumcision was a constant reminder of his covenant relationship with God. This seal became so significant that a Jewish man who did not bear the sign would be cut off from his people. It is also significant that the sign related to a man's sexuality.

According to Colossians chapter 2, baptism serves the same role that circumcision did under the earlier covenant. Through baptism, Christ purifies and prepares our hearts for a relationship with Him. It seals the deal of our profession of faith in Christ as our "old man" is buried and we are resurrected into a new life as new creatures. Communion helps us remember Jesus' atoning death and recall the benefits we have received from His sacrifice. Communion is the sign that we are walking in good faith in our commitment to Him. It releases powerful blessings to us as we take it.

So, sex is far more than an act that simply makes us feel good. It is the sacred covenant seal and sign of our marriages. And it is powerful. It is the most special, spiritual, and powerful aspect of our marriages. The apostle Paul writes:

Do you not know that your bodies are members of Christ? Shall I then take the members of Christ and make *them* members of a harlot? Certainly not! Or do you not know that he who is joined to a harlot is one body *with her?* For *"the two,"* He says, *"shall become one flesh."* But he who is joined to the Lord is one spirit *with Him.* Flee sexual immorality. Every sin that a man does is outside the body, but he who commits sexual immorality sins against his own body. Or do you not know that your body is the temple of the Holy Spirit *who is* in you, whom you have from God, and you are not your own? For you were bought at a price; therefore glorify God in your body and in your spirit, which are God's (1 Corinthians 6:15–20).

Paul wanted the believers in Corinth to know that sex is only for a husband and wife within the covenant of marriage. He also informs them that sex is spiritual because they are individually the temple of the Holy Spirit and one with Jesus. Their bodies no longer belong to them; they belong to Jesus. Marriage is a spiritual union, and sex creates and maintains the deepest possible intimacy when we honor it properly. Paul also lets them know that sex is incredibly powerful. It is so strong that it binds the couple into a single unit as "one."

3. Sex and Soul Ties

When a person engages in sexual intercourse, his or her body releases hundreds of powerful hormones and chemicals. Not only does sexual activity affect our physical bodies, but it also has a deeper spiritual impact. Why is sexual promiscuity so hazardous? It is because when we violate the covenant of marriage, we create dangerous soul ties with other people. Soul ties in and of themselves are not dangerous; some are necessary and beautiful, especially those between a husband and a wife. However, when those ties link us with people who are not our spouses, we create a destructive bond.

In Matthew's gospel, Jesus responds to questions from the Pharisees about marriage and divorce (see Matthew 19:1–10). When asked about divorce, Jesus reminds the Pharisees of God's original intent for marriage as one man and one woman for life. Unsatisfied with His answer, they ask a further question about a man who might want to divorce his wife: "Why then did Moses command to give a certificate of divorce, and to put her away?" (v. 7). Jesus tells them that Moses conceded to divorce in some situations "because of the hardness of your hearts" (v. 8). Finally, Jesus tells them the only acceptable justification for divorce is in the case of adultery. The Greek word for adultery used in the original translation is *porneia*, from which we get our word pornography. It means egregious sexual immorality.

If a spouse commits adultery, it doesn't mean you have to divorce. But if you are married to someone who is a serial, unrepentant cheater, it is certainly grounds for divorce. Why? Because sex is the sacred covenant seal and sign within the marital relationship. It creates such a deep oneness between two people that when we engage in a sexual relationship with someone who is not our spouse, we compromise our own selves as persons and violate the core of our marital bond.

Our souls are the deepest and most sacred parts of our inner beings. When we join with another person in a sexual way, we create a powerful soul bond. In marriage this bond is right, sacred, and beautiful. However, sex outside of marriage causes us to compromise our souls. It makes no difference whether a person is married or unmarried; if we have sex outside of marriage, we are creating a dangerous soul tie. It does not matter whether it is a long-term affair or a five-minute tryst. A bond still exists, although it is much worse if a romantic connection is created in the process.

I often compare this bond with placing duct tape on a carpet and then pulling the tape away from it. You can walk away with all the tape, but you will carry some of the carpet with you. In the same way, when you have a sexual relationship with another person other than your spouse, you can walk away but a part of that person remains with you. Again, in marriage this bond is healthy. However, if someone engages in serial sexual relationships, that person will lose the ability to bond with anyone until there is repentance and the soul ties are broken. One of the surest ways to test whether you still have a soul tie with someone who is not your spouse is to admit if you have chronic romantic and sexual thoughts of others, including boyfriends, girlfriends, or ex-spouses. Or you may have the inability to focus on your spouse and create intimacy, despite your sexual activity. The soul tie must be broken so you can move forward.

(In my book *The Four Laws of Love,* I speak in-depth about how to break soul ties in my chapter on True Sexual Intimacy.)

As I said earlier, this generation is facing serious and novel issues regarding sexual morality that people in previous times could have never imagined. Soul ties related to pornography and lustful fantasies can also occur. In fact, in some cases, they are much worse. Sexuality based on fantasy is ever-present and idealistic. Some people have become so addicted to pornographic and fantasy characters that they visualize them even when they are having sex with their spouses. These soul ties must also be severed.

GOD'S ANSWER TO SEXUAL IMMORALITY

The time is coming when God will no longer allow sexual immorality to run rampant. Just as judgment came in the days of Noah and Lot, God will soon intervene. In the meantime believers should examine themselves. Are we living according to God's design for our sexuality? Now is the time for us to address these sins so we will be ready when He returns. What is God's answer to sexual sin and improper soul ties?

- If there is sexual sin in your life, *repent* of it and receive forgiveness. Repentance means that although you were going one direction, you do a complete about-face and start going God's way. The apostle John reminds us: "If we confess our sins, He is faithful and just to forgive us our sins and to cleanse us from all unrighteousness" (1 John 1:9).

- If *someone has sinned against you,* forgive and bless that person until your heart is healed. Soul ties can even happen in the case of an abuser. They will cause lasting torment until you break them. I am not telling you to excuse the abuse; I am telling you to forgive and move on, for your own sake. Jesus said, "But I say to you who hear: Love your enemies, do good to those who hate you, bless those who curse you, and pray for those who spitefully use you" (Luke 6:27–28).

- If you have been engaged in *sinful conduct,* then *confess* it to your spouse or another trusted, mature believer. Ask for prayer and support. The apostle James told believers, "Confess your trespasses to one another, and pray for one another, that you may be healed" (James 5:16).

- *Break contact* with the person or persons with whom you have shared improper soul ties. If you must have contact because of legal reasons, job duties, shared parental custody, or something of that nature, then make sure your interactions are appropriate and honor God. Clean out all mementos, photographs, letters, or other objects that remind you of that relationship. Once you have broken the tie, don't return to it again.

- As often happens, the person with whom you have broken contact may come to your mind. You may even have temptations related to that individual. In the event these thoughts or feelings occur, *take your thoughts captive* (2 Corinthians 10:5). In other words, catch yourself before you go too far. Immediately confess your struggle to the Lord and another trusted, mature believer and repent of any impure or sinful thoughts. Then replace those thoughts. If you are married, say to yourself, *I am committed to my spouse, and I will place my thoughts on my spouse. I will no longer dwell on someone with whom I should not have a romantic or sexual relationship. That is not God's best for me, and I refuse to listen to the voice of temptation, whether it was birthed by my own flesh or from the devil's lies.* Once you have made that positive confession, fill your mind and heart with the truths of God's Word.

- *Break the soul tie* in the name of Jesus. Consider asking another mature believer to pray along with you. Ask the Holy Spirit to sanctify you—set you apart and cleanse you before God. Tell the Holy Spirit you receive His healing for your soul; it is available to you if you will accept it.

- Agree with the Lord Jesus that you will *dedicate your body and soul* only to Him and to your spouse. If you have done that, then remind yourself that neither your body nor soul are available for anyone else. Recommit and restore the sanctity of your sexual covenant with God and your spouse.

- *Pray with your spouse* about your sexual relationship. Be honest and accountable to both your spouse and God. He will give you the resources you need to stand against temptation and will restore the sanctity of your sexual covenant, but you must allow Him into that area of your life.

This process is not always simple or easy. You may have to repeat it often and over a period of time, depending on the severity of the soul tie. Why is this issue so important and how does it relate to the end times? It is a vital issue for you because sex is extremely special and the most powerful part of a marriage relationship as both a sign and seal. It consummates the relationship and reconfirms the vows you have made. It has the power to release blessings for the good and consequences for the bad. Jesus is coming soon, and He told us that in the days of His return it would be like the days of Noah and Lot. This is exactly what we are seeing today and even worse. But like Noah and Lot, we must not participate in the sins of our generation. Instead, we must live for God and be a chaste Bride for Him when He returns.

TECHNOLOGY AT A TIPPING POINT

8

SILICON VALLEY MEETS THE BIBLE

I want to begin this chapter with a very important reminder. First, the good news: God is in control, not the devil. Second, Jesus is coming, and no one on earth can stop Him. Jesus said, "When these things begin to happen, look up and lift up your heads, because your redemption draws near" (Luke 21:28). So as I write about all of the signs of the end times, hold onto the most important message: Jesus is on His way, and we will soon see the Kingdom of God birthed on this earth with Jesus as its Supreme Ruler. This is all good news. Nevertheless, I want you to recognize that right now we are living in a very severe time. The Bible says this will be an age of unique human technological capabilities, different from any other generation that precedes it. Consider what you have witnessed in only the past decade, and you will recognize the speed at which all of this is happening.

FOUR TECHNOLOGICAL ADVANCEMENTS

The Bible addresses technology far more than many people recognize. I want to tell you about four significant technological advancements the Bible prophesies will happen in the last days.

1. Travel and Knowledge

The angel spoke this to the prophet Daniel:

> But you, Daniel, shut up the words, and seal the book until the time of the end; **many shall run to and fro, and knowledge shall increase** (Daniel 12:4, emphasis added).

The angel told Daniel to seal up the book because no one would understand it until the end times. Then Daniel learned that when the end came "many people will go to and fro, and knowledge shall increase." What does this mean? Both travel and knowledge will increase. Does that apply to our generation? Absolutely! Hundreds of years ago, an average person could only go 20 to 40 miles in a single day, either by foot or on a horse. Occasionally, Karen and I will go that far for dinner.

One of my friends tells about the shock when his grandparents told their parents they would be taking a job and moving seven miles away to the end of the county. Their parents acted as though they were moving to the other side of the world. Today, many people's children actually do live on the other side of the world, and it's not that unusual. But a century ago, it would have been seen with the same fascination that space travel receives today. People couldn't casually travel back then. If they boarded a ship and had favorable winds, they might have been able to travel 100 or 200 miles in a single day.

JESUS IS ON HIS WAY, AND
WE WILL SOON SEE THE
KINGDOM OF GOD BIRTHED
ON THIS EARTH WITH JESUS
AS ITS SUPREME RULER.

Then, in the nineteenth century, train travel arrived and became common, which increased mobility quite a bit. In the early twentieth century, cars and then buses revolutionized travel. Tens of miles turned to hundreds. In the 1960s the average person started to travel by airplane. By now most people have traveled on a plane to some destination, and many have flown to other countries. If I could gather a percentage of my readers who have traveled internationally in the past year, the numbers would be astounding. If I asked that question 200 years ago, most of them wouldn't even be home yet. Now we travel extensively, and we are even learning that commercial space travel may become available in the next few years or decades. So, yes, we have seen people go "to and fro" in our generation. Daniel's prophecy has become a reality in our time.

How has knowledge changed in our lifetime? In 1982 Buckminster Fuller developed the Knowledge Doubling Curve. He estimated that until 1900, human knowledge doubled approximately every century. By World War II a knowledge tsunami hit the world, increasing the rate of doubling to approximately every 25 years. As long as knowledge remained at a steady rate, it was manageable even with occasional challenges. The real challenge occurs when the rate of knowledge growth becomes exponential. In 2020 IBM estimates the rate of knowledge doubling will increase to once every 12 hours.[54]

Why is this phenomenal growth in knowledge happening? There are several reasons. The internet has upended all of our lives. Have you noticed the panic when teenagers (or even adults) lose Wi-Fi connectivity? Within the next year there will be as many as fifty billion interconnected devices on the planet. These devices hold more data than humans have ever created by themselves. Modern data analytics, along with computing technology, allows governments, companies, and organizations to gather data and discover new insights that would have never been available even a decade ago. New inventions and discoveries have grown with astounding speed. According to the US Patent Office, the number of annual patents has increased from 48,971 in 1963 to 339,993 in 2018.[55]

And so have we experienced a dramatic growth of knowledge and increased access to travel in our day that would astound our ancestors. Daniel's prophecy has been fulfilled in our lifetime. If the return of Christ is delayed a few more years, we will be just as amazed as travel and technology continue to evolve.

2. Instant Global Information

When I say the second technological advancement in biblical prophecy is the advent of global satellite television and the internet, you might wonder, *Is Jimmy telling me that satellite TV and the internet are in the Bible?* Believe it or not, I am! Just read this passage from John's Revelation:

> These are the two olive trees and the two lampstands standing before the God of the earth. And if anyone wants to harm them, fire

proceeds from their mouth and devours their enemies. And if anyone wants to harm them, he must be killed in this manner. These
have power to shut heaven, so that no rain falls in the days of their
prophecy; and they have power over waters to turn them to blood,
and to strike the earth with all plagues, as often as they desire.

When they finish their testimony, the beast that ascends out of the
bottomless pit will make war against them, overcome them, and
kill them. And their dead bodies *will lie* in the street of the great
city which is spiritually called Sodom and Egypt, where also our
Lord was crucified. Then *those* from the peoples, tribes, tongues,
and nations will see their dead bodies three-and-a-half days, and
not allow their dead bodies to be put into graves. And those who
dwell on the earth will rejoice over them, make merry, and send
gifts to one another, because these two prophets tormented those
who dwell on the earth (Revelation 11:4–10).

The two witnesses the apostle John sees in his vision are
Enoch and Elijah, which I briefly mentioned in previous chapters. Some Bible teachers believe the two witnesses are Moses
and Elijah, and they could be right. But I believe they are Enoch
and Elijah because these are the only two men in the Old
Testament who didn't die. Instead, they were taken alive by God
to heaven. John says they will live on earth again before they are
finally killed by the Antichrist. Then their dead bodies will lie in
the streets of Jerusalem for three and a half days.

Many people are familiar with John Hagee, the senior pastor of Cornerstone Church in San Antonio, Texas. His father,
William Bythel Hagee, was also a preacher. In the 1920s and

'30s, William preached on the end times, more than a decade before Israel became a modern nation. He announced, "The end cannot come until Israel is a nation, and all the world can see the same thing at the same time." His listeners must have thought this was an unusual pronouncement. How could the whole world possibly witness the same event at the same time?

Of course, William's contention would have been impossible at the time, but fast forward to almost 100 years later. Not only is Israel a nation again, but because of access to satellite television and the internet, we can also see events streamed live to our living rooms and smartphones at the same time as everyone else in the world. If these two witnesses are killed and their bodies lie in the streets, everyone around the globe can certainly see it at the same time today. The apostle John is saying they will be killed and people all around the world will see it together, celebrate, and even send gifts to one another. You know you're unpopular when people send gifts when you die!

When the Antichrist's power is on the rise, Enoch and Elijah will be like a thorn in his side. They will preach the gospel and testify to God's greatness, and supernatural signs and wonders will follow. Then the Antichrist will kill the two men of God because he will hate them so much. Next, John says, "Now after the three-and-a-half days the breath of life from God entered them, and they stood on their feet, and great fear fell on those who saw them" (Revelation 11:11). God is going to resurrect them, and the two prophets will ascend to heaven. Throughout all these events, the entire world will witness the same thing at the same time. That technology is present and readily available right now.

3. Global Financial Control

During the Tribulation the Antichrist will have military might, but the primary method he will use to control the world is through financial power. John writes,

> I saw another beast coming up out of the earth, and he had two horns like a lamb and spoke like a dragon. And he exercises all the authority of the first beast in his presence, and causes the earth and those who dwell in it to worship the first beast, whose deadly wound was healed. He performs great signs, so that he even makes fire come down from heaven on the earth in the sight of men. And he deceives those who dwell on the earth by those signs which he was granted to do in the sight of the beast, telling those who dwell on the earth to make an image to the beast who was wounded by the sword and lived. He was granted *power* to give breath to the image of the beast, that the image of the beast should both speak and cause as many as would not worship the image of the beast to be killed. He causes all, both small and great, rich and poor, free and slave, to receive a mark on their right hand or on their foreheads, and that no one may buy or sell except one who has the mark or the name of the beast, or the number of his name.
>
> Here is wisdom. Let him who has understanding calculate the number of the beast, for it is the number of a man: His number *is* 666 (Revelation 13:11–18).

As long as the world is trading with physical cash, it is impossible for any government, institution, or individual to completely control its flow. However, if someone can create a cashless society, then control can be maintained through a central, electronic data point. We are the world's first generation with a central electronic system, which one person could ultimately control. Granted, multiple servers, systems, and data banks feed into a single system, but they are all interconnected (or if not, the technology is available to do it).

Not long ago, I was on the telephone with one of the credit card companies I use. Karen and I were having a problem with one of our credit cards. The agent on the other end finally said, "Okay, Mr. Evans. It's done." Do you understand the significance of that brief response? The company representative meant the action was applied at that very moment. While I was on the phone, the agent made an adjustment to our account, and it happened in real time. I've been all over the world and used my credit card. With a single swipe or chip insertion, my card is charged, and the sale is recorded within a few seconds. Now I can simply tap my cell phone or card at the point of sale. That technology isn't available everywhere yet, but it soon will be.

Chip technology extends far beyond credit cards. Many people use this technology in their pets. VeriChip is a newer technology. It is an injectable identification chip about the size of a grain of rice and is inserted under the skin to provide biometric verification. It can hold technology and data, including an identification number, an electromagnetic coil for transmitting data, and a tuning capacitor. Its components are enclosed inside a silicon and glass container, which is compatible with biological tissue. Chips aren't used simply to find lost pets any longer. In human use they can be linked to information contained in external databases, which include personal identification, criminal history, and medical information. These chips, which use wireless transmission technology (RFID) can be read by a scanner up to four feet away.[56]

With a chip, anyone could have access to data about you through a centralized data bank. It can include all of your medical and financial information. It can be placed in your arm, on your hand, or even in your forehead. I write this to remind you that the Bible says there will be some kind of identification on the bodies of every individual who wants to buy or sell. If the Tribulation started today, the technology is already available to track and maintain data on every individual in the world. This type of technology that I'm writing about simply did not exist a century ago. Ours is the first generation to experience this kind of technological advancement that the Bible says will be available in the Tribulation.

Whatever form the Mark of the Beast takes, this will be a world where the Church has been removed and the devil incarnate is in charge. If people who remain refuse to receive the mark on their foreheads or hands, then they will be unable to transact business. Even so, the significance of receiving the mark isn't only to empower them to buy or sell. The purpose of the mark is to make sure they conform to the godless ideologies of the Beast, and that is why this sin in unforgiveable.

Even though the Church will have been raptured and will be in heaven at the Marriage Supper of the Lamb, there will still be people on the earth who will have an opportunity to be saved. These people will be persecuted beyond anything any generation has ever seen, beginning with being unable to buy or sell if they refuse the mark. The primary power the Antichrist will have over the world will be financial.

Even now, as you witness or experience the financial pressures that godless forces are exerting to promote their godless beliefs, you are witnessing the spirit of the Antichrist at work. He will not stop until he is in complete control of the world and people everywhere worship him as God. We are living in a critical time when believers must be strong and not bow their knees to these forces. We must stand up for biblical values and be true to our commitment to Christ.

Again, I do not personally know what the mark of the Beast will be. I have read and heard about many theories, and you probably have read some of them as well. This is what the Bible says:

> A third angel followed them, saying with a loud voice, "If anyone worships the beast and his image, and receives *his* mark on his forehead or on his hand, he himself shall also drink of the wine of the

wrath of God, which is poured out full strength into the cup of His indignation. He shall be tormented with fire and brimstone in the presence of the holy angels and in the presence of the Lamb. And the smoke of their torment ascends forever and ever; and they have no rest day or night, who worship the beast and his image, and whoever receives the mark of his name" (Revelation 14:9–11).

Again, the Church on the earth today will not be here during that time. But whoever remains on earth and receives the mark, to that person it is an unforgiveable sin. It will guarantee an eternity in hell.

4. Engineering Humans

Who can forget the spectacular scenes in the 1993 film, *Jurassic Park*? Most moviegoers became so enthralled with the spectacular scenery and the director's interpretation of dinosaurs that they missed how the film is really a critique on genetic engineering. The late Michael Crichton, the author upon whose book the film is based, was himself trained in medical school. Many of his novels address contemporary crises in biomedical technology. In one scene from the movie, Dr. Ian Malcolm (played by Jeff Goldblum) addresses the conscience of the scientific community: "Your scientists were so preoccupied with whether or not they could, they didn't stop to think if they should." In a similar expression of concern, Dr. Malcolm delivers a line that summarizes the entire movie: "God creates dinosaurs. God destroys dinosaurs. God creates man. Man destroys God. Man creates dinosaurs."[57]

Of all the modern technological advances, I believe the most troubling is in the field of genetic engineering—specifically *human* genetic engineering. As with other areas of human knowledge, the technology in the field of genetics and genetic engineering is rapidly increasing. Human genetic modification directly manipulates the human genome using molecular engineering techniques, sometimes called "gene editing." Scientists have divided genetic modification into two types: somatic and germline.

According to the Center for Genetics and Society, somatic modification "adds, cuts, or changes the genes in some of the cells of an existing person, typically to alleviate a medical condition"[58] However, these treatments, while available in some situations, are also very expensive. Germline modification, on the other hand, addresses potential medical conditions in the egg, sperm, or early embryo. These are inherited genes, which scientists attempt to modify before or early after conception. "These alterations would appear in every cell of the person who developed from that gamete or embryo, and also in all subsequent generations."[59]

Scientists and medical ethicists have steered clear of germline modifications because of safety, ethical, and social concerns. In fact, over 40 countries prohibit germline editing, as does an international treaty of the Council of Europe. Still, in January 2014, *Forbes Magazine* declared, "The era of genetically altered humans could begin this year."[60] That statement was only slightly premature. In November 2018, He Jiankui, a Chinese biophysics researcher, announced he had edited the genes of twin girls prior to birth in order to make them more resistant to HIV. The scientific community responded by referring to the "reckless experimentation"[61] as "monstrous" and "unethical." In December 2019, Jiankui received a three-year prison sentence and a high fine.[62]

Most objections from scientists and ethicists are based on the fear of market-based eugenics, meaning people could pay for the kinds of humans they want to create. We can have designer babies. As opposed to allowing nature to run its course, parents may soon be able to choose the gender, height, hair color, and other attributes of their children before they are even conceived or born. For some of us who are older, knowing the gender of a child and having a gender reveal party seems a little newfangled and strange. Just wait until prospective parents can go to a medical office, sit down, and say, "We want this baby to be smart. We want this baby to be tall. We don't want this baby to have any diseases. Here are the diseases of our family. Go in there and change the genetics and erase all this." Humans will be able to play God in some astounding ways. But to paraphrase what Jeff Goldblum's character says in *Jurassic Park,* "You were so preoccupied with whether or not you could, you didn't stop to think if you should."

Another troubling advancement in human engineering is the field of human cloning. The simplest definition is that cloning is the process of creating an identical organism without the involvement of sexual-based reproduction. I'm originally from Amarillo, Texas, which was the home of the American Quarter Horse Association. If you know anything about horse owners, then you understand that breeding is a major concern. When horse breeders want a new colt, they will research family blood-lines and other genetic features. But all of that has changed in recent years. Some have now cloned quarter horses and want to register them with the Association. Clones have been banned since 2004, but there has recently been legal action over whether the Association will be forced to lift that ban.[63]

If it is possible to clone animals, then the next question is what about humans? Various justifications have been used to introduce human cloning into the scientific community. One of them is that it offers humanity a bold step toward immortality. Again, this is a human effort to act in the place of God. I will refer once more to Dr. Malcolm from *Jurassic Park*. Our efforts to replace God in the creation of humans is doomed to failure. There is but one way to ensure immortality, and it comes from embracing God—not replacing Him.

Akin to cloning is the development of human-animal hybrids. By 2011 genetic laboratories in the United Kingdom had produced over 150 hybrids.[64] In June 2019, the Japanese government approved the first human-animal embryo experiments with the hopes of using the resulting hybrids to harvest organs for human transplant.[65] I find these new developments very disturbing. Most of this research is relatively low-tech and can be done all over the world. Human seed is now being introduced into animals. We do not know what the results will be, but throughout the history of the world, nothing like this has happened until now.

Finally, and worst of all, is the human attempt at transhumanism. This scientific manipulation attempts to genetically modify humans and create a new super race for a variety of purposes. I want to remind you again about what I said at the beginning of this chapter: God is in control, and Jesus is coming. Don't forget it.

Many people are familiar with Marvel's Captain America. In this story Steve Rogers is a less than stellar soldier who submits to a biochemical procedure that renders him a super-human specimen and the ultimate fighting machine. His heroic efforts ultimately contribute to the defeat of the Third Reich and a mysterious global conspiracy even more sinister than the Nazis themselves. If you have read the comics or watched the movies about Captain America, you likely considered it an entertaining fantasy with no basis in reality. In recent years, however, some scientific agencies have engaged in research on genetic modification that will enable humans to accomplish what would today be considered superhuman feats.

Although information is tightly guarded, some news outlets have reported that the US government is involved in some of this research, particularly to bolster the physical capabilities of the US fighting forces. I heard former Defense Secretary Chuck Hagel say in a public address, "Russia and China together are doing this also, and right now it's an arms race between us and China and Russia to see who can develop this first." This is a major moment in history, and it is happening now. At the 2015 Exponential Finance conference in New York, Google's director of engineering Ray Kurzweil boldly proclaimed, "Humans will be hybrids by 2030."

> That means our brains will be able to connect directly to the cloud, where there will be thousands of computers, and those computers will augment our existing intelligence. He said the brain will connect via nanobots, tiny robots made from DNA strands. "Our thinking then will be a hybrid of biological and non-biological thinking."[66]

Dedicated transhumanists have referred to the merger of humanity and technology as "singularity."[67] In just a few more decades, transhumanists foresee a new age for humanity, which will include technological developments implanted in human brains and the musculoskeletal system. Anyone who refuses to accept this new reality will be considered "sub-human." They won't be as intelligent or strong and will be susceptible to various diseases, unlike their transhuman counterparts.

THE BELIEVER'S RESPONSE TO TECHNOLOGICAL ADVANCES

I want to end this chapter the way I began. God is in control, and the devil is not. Jesus is coming, and no one on earth can stop Him. Yes, these advances are both interesting and alarming, but don't let human technology distract you from God's superiority. God knew about these things from the beginning. While humans move at lightning speed into the future, remember that God is also Lord of the future. In the next chapter I will address what the Bible has to say about our place in the world and how Christians should respond to the manipulation of human genetics.

9

WHEN THERE ARE
GIANTS IN THE LAND

Much of what I will write in this chapter is absolutely, undeniably true, and I know it. Other things I believe to be true, but only time will tell. I'm not going to mislead you, though. I believe all of it to be the truth as I know it today. If you don't agree with everything I write here, don't get upset. Hang in there because you will find it interesting. I promise I will make a very important statement at the end of the chapter that will tie everything together.

WHO ARE THE GIANTS?

This is what God said to Satan, who was in the form of a serpent, after Adam and Eve sinned:

> Because you have done this,
> You *are* cursed more than all cattle,
> And more than every beast of the field;
> On your belly you shall go,
> And you shall eat dust

All the days of your life.
And I will put enmity
Between you and the woman,
And between your seed and her Seed;
He shall bruise your head,
And you shall bruise His heel (Genesis 3:14–15).

God told the serpent that because he led the human couple into sin, he would have to crawl on his belly. Then the Lord declared a seed war between the devil's seed and God's seed.

A few chapters later, the war took a new twist:

Now it came to pass, when men began to multiply on the face of the earth, and daughters were born to them, that the sons of God saw the daughters of men, that they *were* beautiful; and they took wives of themselves of all they chose.

And the Lord said, "My Spirit shall not strive with man forever, for he *is* indeed flesh; yet his days shall be one hundred and twenty years." There were giants on the earth in those days, and also afterward when the sons of God came in to the daughters of men and they bore *children* to them. These were the mighty men who *were* of old, men of renown.

Then the Lord saw that the wickedness of man *was* great in the earth, and *that* every intent of the thoughts of his heart *was* only evil continually. And the Lord was sorry that He had made man on the earth, and He was grieved in His heart. So the Lord said, "I will destroy man whom I have created from the face of the earth, both man and beast, creeping things, birds of the air. I am sorry that I have made them" (Genesis 6:1–7).

Genesis says that both before and after the Flood, there were giants on earth. The Hebrew word used here for "giants" is the word *nephilim*, which means 'fallen ones.' The Bible says the sons of God had sexual relations with the daughters of men, and they had children, which became known as the fallen ones, or giants. These beings were very different from the humans who descended directly from Adam and Eve. Who, then, are these sons of God Genesis mentions?

Throughout Hebrew and Christian history, many scholars believe Genesis was referring to fallen angels. In the pseudepigraphal book of Enoch, the writer says 200 angels descended upon Mt. Hermon. Then they swore an oath to each other that they would populate the earth by having relations with human women. Incidentally, Mt. Hermon in Hebrew means 'Mountain of the Oath.' Also note, in Deuteronomy chapter 3, when the children of Israel came into the Promised Land, at the foot of Mt. Hermon was a race of giants whom God told the Hebrews to destroy. Goliath and all his relatives would later descend from those giants.

Consider these passages from the book of Job:

There was a day when the sons of God came to present themselves before the Lord, and Satan also came among them. And the Lord said to Satan, "From where do you come?"

So Satan answered the Lord and said, "From going to and fro on the earth, and from walking back and forth on it" (Job 1:6–7).

IN BIBLICAL TERMS HUMANS
ARE IN THE IMAGE OF GOD,
AND GIANTS ARE IN THE
IMAGE OF SATAN.

Again there was a day when the sons of God came to present themselves before the Lord, and Satan came among them also to present
himself before the Lord (Job 2:1).

One thing we can know for certain is that the sons of God
came along with Satan himself to see God. Satan is a fallen angel
who keeps company with fallen angels.

Many Bible scholars have seen this race of giants as the offspring of fallen angels who mated with human women to create
a hybrid race. You may not agree with that assessment, which is
fine. I will add that there is no reference of a biblical giant ever
loving God, just as there is no reference to God ever favoring
a giant. The only certainty is that every time the Bible mentions giants, they are at war with God and God with them. God
utterly destroyed them every time they existed in the Bible. God
destroyed them in the Flood, and then He instructed the children of Israel to rid the land of them under Joshua.

Why did God want to destroy the giants? After all, He loves
humans without measure. However, biblical giants *are* different. They are not humans in the sense of being pure and direct
descendants of Adam and Eve. In biblical terms humans are in
the image of God, and giants are in the image of Satan. This is my
personal position, but it is a studied position.

The Bible repeatedly refers to the physical oddities of these
creatures.

Yet again there was war at Gath, where there was a man of great stature, who had six fingers on each hand and six toes on each foot, twenty-four in number; and he also was born of the giant (2 Samuel 21:20).

That's quite an image. Imagine facing a giant in battle who is waving 12 fingers at you. Also, Deuteronomy gives this record:

Only Og king of Bashan remained of the remnant of the giants. Indeed his bedstead *was* an iron bedstead. (*Is* it not in Rabbah of the people of Ammon?) Nine cubits is its length and four cubits its width, according to the standard cubit (Deuteronomy 3:11).

A conversion of these measurements based on this giant's bed means he was somewhere between 10 and 15 feet tall. His bed was so long that the Ammonites put it on display.

In the book of Numbers, men from Israel were sent to spy out the Promised Land. Ten returned with a terrifying report:

The land through which we have gone as spies *is* a land that devours its inhabitants, and all the people whom we saw in it *are* men of *great* stature. There we saw the giants (the descendants of Anak came from the giants); and we were like grasshoppers in our own sight, and so we were in their sight (Numbers 13:32–33).

Again, the Bible uses the Hebrew word *nephilim* here. They were giants and descendants of Anak, who were also giants. Ten spies returned full of fear and spread that fear among the people.

In the Bible humans seemed fairly normal until the sons of God had relations with the daughters of men. The result was a hybrid race, which God apparently detested. He instructed His people to wipe the giants off the face of the earth.

NOAH, THE "PERFECT" MAN

Returning to Noah, consider this interesting passage from Genesis 6:

> Noah found grace in the eyes of the Lord. This is the genealogy of Noah. Noah was a just man, perfect in his generations. Noah walked with God (vv. 8–9).

At first, this verse seems to contain a contradiction, but I will explain why it does not. First, the writer says Noah found grace in God's eyes. Then he says Noah was "perfect in his generations." How can both of these be true? A perfect person would not need grace. Grace is necessary for us because we are sinners and, therefore, imperfect. Was Noah imperfect and in need of grace, or was he perfect with no need for grace? Regardless of your answer, God saw Noah needed grace and then extended it to him.

If the Bible is without error or contradiction, how do we reconcile this verse? First, the Hebrew word translated "perfect" does not mean Noah was morally perfect; he was a sinner just like you or me. The verse says he was "perfect in his generations," which means he descended from perfect seed. I believe one of the reasons Noah and his family were spared was because they were genetically perfect. They did not come from the serpent's seed, as the giants had. They had not been infected by this hybrid race. As a result, God gave grace to Noah. Although he was an imperfect and sinful human, he was nevertheless fully human. His genetics were without taint or flaw. So God rescued Noah and his family, but He destroyed the race of the giants. After the Flood, Satan and his fallen angels began again, and the seed war continued. David killed the nine-foot tall Goliath in the Valley of Elah, but Goliath had brothers. David and his mighty men had to kill them too.

Two additional passages of Scripture are pertinent to this subject. Peter writes this about the angels who sinned:

> If God did not spare the angels who sinned, but cast *them* down to hell and delivered *them* into chains of darkness, to be reserved for judgment; and did not spare the ancient world, but saved Noah, *one* of eight *people*, a preacher of righteousness, bringing in the flood on the world of the ungodly; and turning the cities of Sodom and Gomorrah into ash, condemned *them* to destruction, making *them* an example to those who would afterward live ungodly (2 Peter 2:4–6).

Jude gives this similar account:

> The angels who did not keep their proper domain, but left their own abode, He has reserved in everlasting chains under darkness for judgment of the great day; as Sodom and Gomorrah, and the cities around them in a similar manner to these, having given themselves over to sexual immorality and gone after strange flesh, are set forth as an example, suffering the vengeance of eternal fire (Jude 1:6–7).

Once again, throughout Jewish and Christian history, scholars held these beliefs about the relationship between the fallen angels and the giants. Those sinful angels came down to earth, where they spawned a hybrid race with human women. God detested that race, and every time He saw it, He destroyed it or commanded its destruction.

I bring all of this to your attention because I believe a hybrid race is being created in the present age. Do you recall what Jesus said? "As the days of Noah *were,* so also will the coming of the Son of Man be" (Matthew 24:37). Jesus was referring to some of the events we know about in this corrupt and immoral world that treats sin as "business as usual." But could He also be referring to the demonic attraction humans have to altering their genetic line once again through methods such as cloning, genetic modification, and transhumanism?

WHOSE IMAGE?

Here is the very important statement I promised to make at the end of this chapter: **Human seed is sacred**. We are made in the image of God, and we have no right to try to improve upon or manipulate what He has done. Yes, good people can access medical technology to help or cure others. However, arrogant humans should not try to take the place of God in an attempt to improve and immortalize themselves. There is only one God, and we are not Him. Human seed should be left untouched.

WE ARE MADE IN THE IMAGE
OF GOD, AND WE HAVE NO
RIGHT TO TRY TO IMPROVE
UPON OR MANIPULATE
WHAT HE HAS DONE.

TIME AT A TIPPING POINT

1 0

GOD IS THE LORD
OF TIME

A few years ago I was preaching about the end times, and a young man approached me between services for advice. He began, "At my place of work, they have a 401(k) that they're asking me to contribute to." Then he asked, "What should I do?" In light of the Second Coming of Jesus, he wondered if he should contribute to his retirement plan. How would you answer? I will tell you how I responded, but first, let me relate a story to you.

HOW TO PREPARE FOR THE SECOND COMING

On May 19, 1780, a strange event occurred in the northeastern United States. Historians refer to this incident as "the Dark Day." On that morning the sky became so dark that it appeared as though day had become night. Birds went back to their nests, and farm animals reacted in terror. Gathering with his troops in south New Jersey, General George Washington wrote about the event in his diary. Northward in Connecticut, all commerce and work ceased as panic grew among the citizens. The people speculated about the cause. Was it an eclipse? Or something else? Some of the Puritan Christians began to think they might be experiencing the judgment of God. A few wondered if this might be the first sign of the Second Coming of Christ.

Meanwhile, the Connecticut legislature was in session, and the delegates became equally uneasy. Some of the members were terrified, thinking the day of judgment was upon them. Finally, one legislator stood and made the motion to adjourn, so they could all return to their houses and prepare for the end of the world. At this point, Abraham Davenport, a sixty-five year old Stamford legislator, spoke against the motion:

> The day of judgment is either approaching, or it is not. If it is not, there is no cause of an adjournment; if it is, I choose to be found doing my duty. I wish therefore that candles may be brought.

At Davenport's urging, candles were brought into the chamber, and the meeting continued. The people's admiration for him as a leader with courage and resolve grew after this event. John Greenleaf Whittier later penned a poem in Davenport's honor.

Shortly thereafter this event, Davenport served as Chief Justice for the Court of Common Pleas in Danbury, Connecticut. As God's providence would have it, he died of a heart attack while presiding over a court case. He met the Lord while doing his duty. As it turns out, "the Dark Day" wasn't a sign from God at all. Rather, it was the smoke from forest fires in Canada wafting southward into New England.[68]

So what did I tell the young man who wondered about his 401(k)? I told him to plan as though Jesus is not returning for a hundred years and live as though Jesus is returning today. I would leave the same message to you. Plan your life. Go to school. Get married. Have children. Give generously. Spend wisely. Save responsibly. Plan for your retirement. God wants you to live your life for His honor and glory but also with a constant awareness that Jesus may return at any moment.

DISCERNING THE TIMES

I want you to be able to discern these very unusual times. If you don't understand them, then you may give in to fear, confusion, and poor preparation. I will say again that I believe we are at the *end* of the end times, which is also the end of the age. We are almost out of time. But why us? And why now? For what reason has God chosen us to be the generation at the end?

From the very beginning of Creation, the Lord laid out how much time He would allot to human history, and we are at the end of that allotment. God is not arbitrary with His plans. The end is not coming because of anything humanity has done. We are so much better and so much worse than generations who have gone before us. Even so, it is God who keeps a master calendar and master clock. We only happen to be the people living on earth when those run out.

GOD WANTS YOU TO LIVE
YOUR LIFE FOR HIS HONOR
AND GLORY BUT ALSO WITH
A CONSTANT AWARENESS
THAT JESUS MAY RETURN
AT ANY MOMENT.

The apostle Peter delivered some very specific prophetic words about the end times:

> Beloved, I now write to you this second epistle (in *both* of which I stir up your pure minds by way of reminder), that you may be mindful of the words which were spoken before by the holy prophets, and of the commandment of us, the apostles of the Lord and Savior, knowing this: that scoffers will come in the last days, walking according to their own lusts, and saying, "Where is the promise of His coming? For since the fathers fell asleep, all things continue as *they were* from the beginning of creation." For this they willfully forget: that by the word of God the heavens were of old, and of the earth standing out of water and in the water, by which the world *that* then existed perished, being flooded with water. But the heaven and the earth *which* are now preserved by the same word, are reserved for fire until the day of judgment and perdition of ungodly men.
>
> But, beloved, do not forget this one thing, that with the Lord one day *is* as a thousand years, and a thousand years is as one day. The Lord is not slack concerning *His* promise, as some count slackness, but is longsuffering toward us, not willing that any should perish but that all should come to repentance (2 Peter 3:1–9).

Peter reminded his readers of the words of the Old Testament prophets. Then he proceeded to a very specific prophecy concerning the end times. When the end comes, he says, there will be mockers scoffing about the last days. When they read or hear teachings like those in this book, they will ridicule them, because they have given into their own lusts. Peter is not writing about godly people; these are unsaved and immoral individuals. He says they will mock these teachings and say, "Nothing has ever changed. Everything has always been the same since the beginning." And Peter says, "Of course, that prophecy has been fulfilled. We know that's true. They willfully reject the authority of the Word of God and the warnings concerning their judgment."

Peter is not writing about people who have not heard or understood these teachings. No, they *willfully* reject them. These individuals have made a conscious decision to close their eyes and ears to God's Word, in the same way people did during the time of Noah. Then the Flood came. In the case of the present world, it is being preserved until it will be consumed by fire. Peter says the people he is writing about will be judged one day.

Then the apostle takes a sharp, unexpected turn. He tells them to remember one very important thing: "With the Lord, one day *is* as a thousand years, and a thousand years as one day" (v. 8). This is a very important concept for us to understand. God sees a day as a thousand years and a thousand years as a day. Peter is referring to a verse from Psalms:

> For a thousand years in Your sight
> *Are* like yesterday when it is past,
> And *like* a watch in the night (Psalm 90:4).

Take note again that Peter is writing about the end times, and he is saying to his readers, "God isn't playing around. He isn't waiting for some arbitrary date before Jesus returns. God is not disorganized. He has a plan. But remember, God's plan doesn't look like human plans. He considers one day on the same scale as a thousand years, and a thousand years as a single day."

God has His own calendar and keeps His own personal planner. He's been carefully following that planner since time began, and He's still watching His calendar. This may be a new way of thinking for you, but it is definitely not a new teaching. The original Jewish readers who were trained in Jewish synagogue schools understood God's timing. Rabbis and Hebrew scholars taught about God's calendar for centuries, and the early church adopted these beliefs.

THE WAY GOD KEEPS TIME

Yes, God has a personal calendar, but He allows His followers to look at it for their benefit.

> Remember the former things of old,
> For I *am* God, and there *is* no other;
> *I am* God, and *there is* none like Me,
> Declaring the end from the beginning,
> And from ancient times *things* that are not *yet* done,
> Saying, "My counsel shall stand,
> And I will do all My pleasure" (Isaiah 46:9-10).

God revealed His calendar in Genesis. This is what the Jewish rabbis taught throughout the years. God has His own way of counting time, and it goes all the way back to the dawn of Creation.

Even though God is mysterious, He does not want us to remain in the dark. He does nothing until He reveals it first. All of human history is about God continually revealing Himself to those who want to know Him. The God of the Bible is not a secret keeper. He does not relish hiding things from us. God is light, and He wants us to live in His light. The reason God gives us prophecy in the Bible is so we will be prepared for everything that will happen. The prophet Amos wrote,

> Surely the Lord God does nothing,
> Unless He reveals His secret to His servants the prophets (3:7).

Bible prophecy isn't just for preachers or experts. God authored it for you, so you would know and be prepared. He doesn't want us to be a fearful and confused people. God wants His children to be informed so they will face the future with courage and certainty.

As I said before, every chapter in 1 Thessalonians addresses the return of Christ. In chapter 5 Paul specifically addresses the issue of time:

> But concerning the times and seasons, brethren, you have no need that I should write you. For you yourselves perfectly know that the day of the Lord so comes as a thief in the night. For when they say, "Peace and safety!" then sudden destruction comes upon them, as labor pains upon a pregnant woman. And they shall not escape. But you, brethren, are not in darkness, so that this Day should overcome you as a thief. You are sons of light and sons of the day. We are not of the night nor of darkness (vv. 1–5).

ALL OF HUMAN HISTORY IS
ABOUT GOD CONTINUALLY
REVEALING HIMSELF TO THOSE
WHO WANT TO KNOW HIM.

Did you realize that every time the Bible speaks about Jesus coming like a thief in the night, it is a message for unbelievers— not believers? Yes, believers should be aware so they can lovingly warn non-believers. But Jesus does not sneak up on believers. God gave the prophecies of the Bible to us so we will be prepared for Jesus' return. We may not know the exact day or hour when He's coming, but we know the seasons. We know the signs of the time. When Jesus comes, we will have our heads lifted up and ready for our Bridegroom.

GOD'S 7,000-YEAR CALENDAR

In the Bible God counts time in sevens. In Genesis 1 He takes seven days to create the world. Then in Leviticus chapter 25, God tells the Hebrew people to mark every seventh year as a Sabbath year, during which they are to let the land rest and plant nothing. At the end of seven Sabbath years, they are to commemorate with the Year of Jubilee. In Daniel's prophecy God declared 490 prophetic years to the nation of Israel. In Daniel chapter 9, the angel spoke to Daniel and told him that Israel would be given these 70 x 7 years, and then the end would come.

Throughout the centuries many Jewish scholars taught that the seven days in Genesis chapter 1 correspond to 7,000 years of human history. In the very beginning, God was saying, "There will be 7,000 years for humanity." During the first 6,000 years, humans will have an opportunity to manage the earth. Then Christ will reign on earth for 1,000 years.

Humanity's 6,000 years are over. This timing isn't arbitrary, and it's not because of anything humans have done. At the very beginning of Creation, God started His clock. We simply happen to be the generation that is alive at its fulfillment. I am going to demonstrate this timeline for you in three ways.

1. The Days of Creation and the Seven Millennium

First, I want to show you how the seven days of Creation prophetically parallel each of the seven millennia of human history.

DAY ONE: LIGHT SEPARATES FROM DARKNESS (GENESIS 1:3–5)

On the first day of Creation, God separated light from darkness. Then the sins of the first humans, Adam and Eve, separated them from the God of light. Light and darkness were separated physically and then spiritually. This was the most significant event in the first thousand years of human history.

DAY TWO: THE WATERS ABOVE AND BELOW SEPARATE (GENESIS 1:6–10)

On the second day God separated the waters above from the waters below. In the second human millennium, God accessed the waters above and below as a judgment in the Flood. God brought the waters together, flooded the earth, and then He separated them again, just as He did on the second day of the Creation.

DAY THREE: SEED-BEARING PLANTS BEGIN TO FILL THE EARTH WITH LIFE (GENESIS 1:11–13)

On the third day God created plants with seeds. For the first time, the earth had life. In the third millennium of human history, the Lord made a lasting promise to Abraham that through his seed, all the nations of the earth would be blessed.

DAY FOUR: LIGHTS FILL THE SKY (GENESIS 1:14–19)

On the fourth day God made lights to fill the sky: the sun, moon, and stars. In the fourth millennium, God raised up prophets to give light to Israel. Then God sent His Son Jesus as the Light of the World.

DAY FIVE: LIVING ANIMALS CREATED (GENESIS 1:20–23)

On the fifth day God created the first living creatures. In the fifth millennium of human history, God raised up new creatures who would inherit eternal life because of Christ's life, death, and resurrection.

DAY SIX: HUMANS CREATED AS THE CROWN OF GOD'S CREATION (GENESIS 1:26–28)

On the sixth day God created man and woman. He told them to fill the earth and subdue it. The sixth millennium is the one in which we are now living. God has empowered the Church to grow and take authority in the world, just as He did for Adam and Eve. They failed in God's commands, but by the Holy Spirit, He has empowered us to accomplish what He originally called them to do.

DAY SEVEN: GOD RESTED

After God created everything, He rested on the seventh day. In the seventh millennium God will restore the earth, and all humanity will rest with Jesus as our ruler for the next thousand years.

The apostle John describes this thousand-year reign of Christ:

Then I saw an angel coming down from heaven, having the key to the bottomless pit and a great chain in his hand. He laid hold of the dragon, that serpent of old, who is *the* Devil and Satan, and bound him for a thousand years; and he cast him into the bottomless pit, and shut him up, and set a seal on him, so that he should deceive the nations no more till the thousand years were finished. But after these things he must be released for a little while.

And I saw thrones, and they sat on them, and judgment was committed to them. Then *I saw* the souls of those who had been beheaded for their witness to Jesus and for the word of God, who had not worshiped the beast or his image, and had not received *his* mark on their foreheads or on their hands. And they lived and reigned with Christ for a thousand years. But the rest of the dead did not live again until the thousand years were finished. This *is* the first resurrection. Blessed and holy *is* he who has part in the first resurrection. Over such the second death has no power, but they shall be priests of God and of Christ, and shall reign with Him a thousand years (Revelation 20:1–6).

From this passage in Revelation, we are assured of the certainty of the last thousand years of human history as the millennial rule of Jesus Christ. We are now living before the Rapture and the Tribulation. The next major event will be the Rapture of the Church. Soon thereafter, the world will experience seven years of tribulation. During that same seven year period, believers will be experiencing a wedding with Jesus in heaven. (Incidentally, a traditional Jewish wedding lasts seven days.)

WHAT WILL HAPPEN AFTER THE END?

At the end of the seven-year Marriage Supper of the Lamb and the Tribulation, which you can read about in Revelation chapters 19 and 20, Jesus will return again. We, as His Bride, will return with Him. He will defeat the Antichrist and false prophet, throwing them into the lake of fire. Satan will be bound and thrown into a bottomless pit for 1,000 years. Then Jesus will establish His millennial kingdom. He will be the Supreme Ruler on earth, and His people will rule and reign with Him. No one will be able to overthrow Him, and He will never need to be reelected.

At the end of that thousand years, Satan will be loosed once again. Believers who have been reigning with Christ are immortal. However, Satan will gather the mortals who remain on earth to march on Jerusalem. The Bible says Satan will lead Gog and Magog, which are symbolic of the nations of the world, in a rebellion against Jesus. Their march to Jerusalem is really an attempt to kill Jesus once again.

Jesus will then slay them all and commence with the Great White Throne Judgment, in which He will judge all of the dead from the very beginning of time. Then the heavens and the earth will be destroyed by fire, which is what Peter was writing about. God will create new heavens and a new earth. When He does, the New Jerusalem will descend from heaven. This city will be approximately 1,280 miles in length, breadth, and height (Revelation 21:16). This will be the place where we will live with Jesus for all eternity. It will be more wonderful than any of us can imagine.

2. Counting the Years

Another way to look at human history is by simply counting the years. If we are in the end times and human history is a period of 6,000 years, then a survey of the calendar will give us verification that we are very near the end. I will demonstrate three calendars that substantiate what I am writing here.

THE GREGORIAN CALENDAR

The year of this book's publication is AD 2020 on the Gregorian calendar. The abbreviation AD stands for the Medieval Latin term *anno domini,* which is translated as "the year of the Lord." The complete original phrase was *anno domini nostril Jesu Christi*—"in the year of our Lord Jesus Christ." In his gospel Luke includes a genealogy that extends from Jesus all the way back to Adam (3:23–38). From this account we can know precisely the number of generations from Adam until Jesus. Most Old Testament scholars agree that the history of the Old Testament covers a period of approximately 4,000 years. With approximately 2,000 years from Jesus' earthly ministry until the present, human history is currently about 6,000 years old.

THE JEWISH CIVIL CALENDAR

The Jewish people have historically maintained two calendars, one civil and the other religious. According to the Jewish civil calendar, the year of this book's publication is 5780. Since they include neither AD nor BC in their calendar, the first year extends all the way to Creation. So if the year is 5780, then 20 years remain until the 6,000-year mark. There is some dispute regarding the accuracy of this calendar, but even with variances and discrepancies, the total years still remain approximately 6,000.

THE JEWISH RELIGIOUS CALENDAR

In the Jewish civil calendar, a new year commences in the fall, but in the religious calendar, it starts in the spring. A small group of Messianic Jews do not give credence to the civil calendar.[69] Through exhaustive research they maintain that 6,000 years from Creation is much closer to the present year. They also believe in a 7,000-year human history, but they dispute some of the dates held by others. They have also made a few adjustments to their own dates since I first discovered them. For example, they originally said 2015 was year 6001 and speculated that Jesus would be returning that September. However, as we know, Jesus did not return then. So I'm giving caution to anyone who is looking for a specific date.

WHY I DON'T SET SPECIFIC DATES

I take this position for two reasons. First, when some well-meaning people set dates, others shirk their responsibilities and stop living their lives. Second, when an advertised date comes and goes, people who have placed their faith in the date become disappointed and cynical. Skeptics use it as a foil for ridicule. Over my lifetime, I have witnessed many people who set dates. I do not recall the results being good for any of those people. Whenever someone tells me they know precisely when Jesus is coming, I have a ready answer: "I hope you're right. But I'm not going to live any differently just because you say you know the exact day."

3. Biblical Symbols

Prophetic symbols in the Bible are another way we can measure the 7,000-year span of human history.

THE NOAH CONNECTION

In Luke's gospel Jesus says,

> As it was in the days of Noah, so it will be also in the days of the Son of Man: They ate, they drank, they married wives, they were given in marriage, until the day that Noah entered the ark, and the flood came and destroyed them all (Luke 17:26–27).

Jesus draws a direct parallel between Noah and His Second Coming. Noah lived to the age of 950 years, according to Genesis 9:29. Jesus said the world would be like the time of Noah when He returns.

God could have placed Noah on the ark at any point in Noah's life. However, Genesis 7:6 says, "Noah was six hundred years old when the floodwaters were on the earth." A few verses later, we read:

> In the six hundredth year of Noah's life, in the second month, the seventeenth day of the month, on that day all the fountains of the great deep were broken up, and the windows of heaven were opened. And the rain was on the earth forty days and forty nights (Genesis 7:11–12).

Out of Noah's 950 years, God chose the year 600. Human history will last 6,000 years, followed by the thousand-year rule of Christ. Could Noah's age at the Flood be symbolic for Jesus' return to rescue His people in 6,000 years?

THE WEDDING AT CANA

I want to show you one more symbolic biblical parallel. When Jesus was 12 years old, He went with His family to Jerusalem for Passover. When the feast was over, His parents (Mary and Joseph) started the journey home, not knowing Jesus had stayed behind at the Temple. Soon Mary and Joseph realized Jesus was not in their traveling party, and they began to search frantically for Him. They found Jesus three days later, and His explanation was, "Did you not know that I must be about My Father's business?" (Luke 2:49). Still, Jesus went home to Nazareth with His parents. Mary's unspoken (and possibly spoken) message was that Jesus was not yet ready to embark on His public ministry.

Seventeen years later, at a wedding in Cana of Galilee, God used Mary to deliver a different message. The host ran out of wine, and Mary relayed the problem to Jesus. He replied, "What does your concern have to do with Me? My hour has not yet come" (John 2:4). Mary turned to the servants and said, "Whatever He says to you, do *it*" (John 2:5). This simple instruction was a direct affirmation of Jesus' authority and signaled the start of His public ministry.

Now there were set there six waterpots of stone, according to the manner of purification of the Jews, containing twenty or thirty gallons apiece. Jesus said to them, "Fill the waterpots with water." And they filled them up to the brim. And He said to them, "Draw *some* out now, and take *it* to the master of the feast." And they took *it*. When the master of the feast had tasted the water that was made wine, and did not know where it came from (but the servants who had drawn the water knew), the master of the feast called the bridegroom. And he said to him, "Every man at the beginning sets out the good wine, and when the *guests* have well drunk, then the inferior. You have kept the good wine until now!" This beginning of signs Jesus did in Cana of Galilee (John 2:6–11).

John wrote that Jesus' turning water into wine was the beginning of the *signs* in His ministry. There are important distinctions between miracles, signs, and wonders. Miracles happen when God does something supernaturally that only He can do. Wonders fill those who witness them with awe and amazement. Signs, however, point to something other than themselves for meaning. While this act by Jesus was miraculous and wonderful, the meaning was much deeper. This was the beginning of Jesus' ministry, and God was revealing an important sign. He was declaring the end from the beginning.

What was Jesus doing at the very beginning of His ministry? He was at a wedding, serving heaven's wine. Now I want to make an important connection. What did Jesus do at the very end of His ministry, and what will He do when He comes again to take us to be with Him? He did—and will—serve us heaven's wine. In Matthew 26 Jesus told His disciples, "I will not drink of this fruit of the vine from now on until that day when I drink it new with you in My Father's kingdom" (v. 29). Many believe the six water pots represent the 6,000 years of human history, which will end with believers at a wedding, drinking heaven's wine with Jesus.

WHEN IT ALL COMES TO PASS

When I say I believe we are living in the end times, I am not offering pure speculation. I'm not merely guessing. Throughout this book I have been demonstrating why I believe the Bible says the end of the end times is already here and advancing rapidly. Whether I have shown this to you through Israel, a falling away from the truth, the advances in technology, the way the calendar corresponds to Bible prophecy, or something else, I am basing my observations on what I read in the Bible.

God's 7,000-year calendar has been present since the very beginning, and that's what many Jewish and Christian scholars have believed for centuries. When the apostle Peter wrote to the Church about the end times, he told them they could be certain that when the end came, people would mock teachings about it. They will willfully reject the authority of the Word of God and ignore the warnings concerning the judgment that is coming on the world. Then he told them to remember one very important fact: with the Lord, one day is as 1,000 years, and 1,000 years is as one day.

God isn't stalling or delaying needlessly. In the present time He is offering every living person an opportunity to repent and believe. That is why I told the young man who approached me about his 401(k) to live his life to the glory of God. Time is short, and God is looking for people who will be living their lives for Him and be prepared when He returns.

11

WHAT TIME IS IT?

I am asked on a regular basis what I believe about where we are currently on God's prophetic clock. This has even become more common since the outbreak of the worldwide coronavirus pandemic. In fact, one man asked me if I thought we were now experiencing the four horsemen of Revelation chapter six. I told him that I didn't believe any of the events we are experiencing have anything to do with the Tribulation chapters of the book of Revelation. Let me explain my reasoning.

Jesus spoke often and explicitly about the end times, and we should be especially grateful for that in the times in which we are living. Let me show you several important passages that reveal to us where we are on God's prophetic clock. And let me tell you in advance—it is both comforting and encouraging. Even though we are definitely living in difficult and tumultuous times, the words of Jesus give us great hope.

A passage that I've already talked about in this book has some very important insight for us regarding the times we are living in, as well as the timing of the Rapture of the Church. It is found in the seventeenth chapter of the book of Luke:

> Then He said to the disciples, "The days will come when you will desire to see one of the days of the Son of Man, and you will not see *it*. And they will say to you, 'Look here!' or 'Look there!' Do not go after *them* or follow *them*. For as the lightning that flashes out of one *part* under heaven shines to the other *part* under heaven, so also the Son of Man will be in His day. But first He must suffer many things and be rejected by this generation. And as it was in the days of Noah, so it will be also in the days of the Son of Man: **They ate, they drank, they married wives, they were given in marriage, until the day that Noah entered the ark, and the flood came and destroyed them all**. Likewise as it was also in the days of Lot: **They ate, they drank, they bought, they sold, they planted, they built; but on the day that Lot went out of Sodom it rained fire and brimstone from heaven and destroyed *them* all. Even so will it be in the day when the Son of Man is revealed**.
>
> In that day, he who is on the housetop, and his goods *are* in the house, let him not come down to take them away. And likewise the one who is in the field, let him not turn back. Remember Lot's wife. Whoever seeks to save his life will lose it, and whoever loses his life will preserve it. I tell you, in that night there will be two *men* [or people] in one bed: the one will be taken and the other will be left. Two *women* will be grinding together: the one will be taken and the other left. Two *men* will be in the field: the one will be taken and the other left."
>
> And they answered and said to Him, "Where, Lord?" So He said to them, "Wherever the body is, there the eagles will be gathered together" (Luke 17:22–37, emphasis added).

According to Jesus, the days prior to the Rapture of the Church and the beginning of the Tribulation will be marked by a business as usual atmosphere. There will be "buying and selling," meaning that there will be general economic stability. Even though there are times of economic instability such as we saw in 2008 and more recently related to the coronavirus panic, these are just temporary economic events. Based on the words of Jesus, I want to tell you with authority that there will not be a worldwide economic collapse prior to the Rapture.

It is always wise to prepare ourselves for the inevitable ups and downs of life. But there is no need to hoard or build a survival bunker. Those are things that people who don't know the Lord or Bible prophecy do out of fear and ignorance. However, we are to be a people of faith who know our God. And He would never leave us unprepared if there was going to be a cataclysmic financial collapse.

Notice in the passage from Luke that Jesus says His return for the Church will be just like **the day** Noah and his family got onto the Ark, **before** the judgment of God fell. Jesus repeats this point regarding Lot: "**On the day** that Lot went out of Sodom it rained fire and brimstone from heaven and destroyed *them* all. Even so will it be in **the day** when the Son of Man is revealed" (Luke 17:29–30, emphasis added). Jesus isn't speaking about a season of time—He is referring to an actual day in history that is recorded in the Bible. He is clearly connecting one single day in Lot's life to one single day when He will rapture the Church, and then judgment will fall on the earth. Also notice that Jesus refers to "in that day" and also "in that night." The reason this is important is because when the Rapture occurs, half of the world will be in daytime and the other half will be in nighttime. So, whatever time of the day it occurs, we should always be watchful.

We are definitely living in a very immoral, violent, and rebellious world, just as Noah and Lot experienced. But we are also living in the days prior to the Rapture where there is a business as usual atmosphere that will remain until we are taken out. Then all heaven will break loose, and true judgment will come on the earth. But we won't be here for that—praise the Lord!

Let me show you another important text that helps us understand the times we are living in.

> Now as He sat on the Mount of Olives, the disciples came to Him privately, saying, "Tell us, when will these things be? And what *will be* the sign of Your coming, and of the end of the age?" And Jesus answered and said to them: "Take heed that no one deceives you. For many will come in My name, saying, 'I am the Christ,' and will deceive many. And you will hear of wars and rumors of wars. See that you are not troubled; for all *these things* must come to pass, but the end is not yet. For nation will rise against nation, and kingdom against kingdom. And there will be famines, pestilences, and earthquakes in various places. All these *are* the beginning of sorrows" (Matthew 24:3–8).

I believe that for the past seventy-plus years since Israel became a nation in 1948, we have been experiencing all of the signs Jesus gave in this passage. Therefore, I believe we are in the time of "the beginning of sorrows." I also believe that these signs are intensifying, like labor pains that are announcing the birth of a child. The worldwide coronavirus outbreak is just one example of the pestilences that have been plaguing the world for some time now. And let me repeat again: every generation has had some of the signs that Jesus mentioned. But we are experiencing every sign!

One more important text concerning the end times is found later in Matthew 24, where Jesus speaks about the signs of the end:

> Now learn this parable from the fig tree: When its branch has already become tender and puts forth leaves, you know that summer *is* near. So you also, when you see all these things, know that it is near—at the doors! **Assuredly, I say to you, this generation will by no means pass away till all these things take place.** Heaven and earth will pass away, but My words will by no means pass away (Matthew 24:32–35, emphasis added).

What Jesus is telling us here is that one generation will see all end times events fulfilled.

He couldn't have been speaking of His generation because they all died. He was speaking of the generation that would witness the signs of which He was speaking. So, as I've said earlier in the book, God's prophetic end times clock started ticking in 1948 when Israel became a nation. This is clear in this passage from the book of Joel:

For behold, in those days and at that time,

When I bring back the captives of Judah and Jerusalem,

I will also gather all nations,

And bring them down to the Valley of Jehoshaphat;

And I will enter into judgment with them there

On account of My people, My heritage Israel,

Whom they have scattered among the nations;

They have also divided up My land (Joel 3:1–2).

In this passage God links two events together into the same time sequence. He reveals to us that in the same time period in which He regathers Israel back into her land, He will also enter into a final judgment with all nations regarding their mistreatment of the Jews and for dividing the land (which the UN and the US have forced Israel to do). According to Joel chapter three, the regathering of the Jews to the land of Israel started God's prophetic clock and also the final generation.

Here's a very important question to ask: how long is a generation? To answer that question, let me tell you about an important principle of biblical interpretation. **The Bible must interpret itself.** In other words, to find out how long a generation is, we need to find out what the Bible has to say about it first and foremost. And here is what the Bible says about a generation:

The days of our lives *are* seventy years;

And if by reason of strength *they are* eighty years,

Yet their boast *is* only labor and sorrow;

For it is soon cut off, and we fly away (Psalm 90:10).

Since Israel became a nation in 1948, more than 70 years have passed. This is why I not only believe we are living in the end times, but I also believe we are living in the *end* of the end times. Before going any further I want you to know that I never set dates, and I don't want to encourage you to do this either. In making this point about one generation witnessing all end times events, someone might think that I'm saying the Rapture has to happen and Armageddon has to occur no later than May 14, 2028. I'm not saying that.

But I am saying I believe it will happen around this time period. And the only way that it won't is if I'm wrong about a generation being 70 or 80 years long. Based on Scripture, though, I feel confident about that time period. Also, we are seeing so many end times events being fulfilled or getting ready to be fulfilled. Just look at what is happening in Israel alone. And we must always remember that Israel and Jerusalem are ground zero for Bible prophecy.

There is something else I want to say about one generation seeing all things fulfilled related to end times prophecy. And this takes things to an entirely different level regarding the Rapture of the Church. We need to understand that when Jesus said one generation would see all things fulfilled, He was including in that statement the Tribulation and Second Coming. Look at this text from Matthew chapter 24 that precedes Jesus' promise of a one generation event:

"Therefore when you see the 'abomination of desolation,' spoken of by Daniel the prophet, standing in the holy place" (whoever reads, let him understand), "then let those who are in Judea flee to the mountains. Let him who is on the housetop not go down to take anything out of his house. And let him who is in the field not go back to get his clothes. But woe to those who are pregnant and to those who are nursing babies in those days! And pray that your flight may not be in winter or on the Sabbath. For then there will be great tribulation, such as has not been since the beginning of the world until this time, no, nor ever shall be. And unless those days were shortened, no flesh would be saved; but for the elect's sake those days will be shortened.

Then if anyone says to you, 'Look, here *is* the Christ!' or 'There!' do not believe *it*. For false christs and false prophets will rise and show great signs and wonders to deceive, if possible, even the elect. See, I have told you beforehand.

Therefore if they say to you, 'Look, He is in the desert!' do not go out; or 'Look, *He is* in the inner rooms!' do not believe it. For as the lightning comes from the east and flashes to the west, so also will the coming of the Son of Man be. For wherever the carcass is, there the eagles will be gathered together.

Immediately after the tribulation of those days the sun will be darkened, and the moon will not give its light; the stars will fall from heaven, and the powers of the heavens will be shaken. Then the sign of the Son of Man will appear in heaven, and then all the tribes of the earth will mourn, and they will see the Son of Man coming on the clouds of heaven with power and great glory. And He will send His angels with a great sound of a trumpet, and they will gather together His elect from the four winds, from one end of heaven to the other" (Matthew 24:15–31).

This passage gives a fuller understanding of all of the events Jesus includes in His promise that one generation will see all things fulfilled. And He speaks of the abomination of desolation that occurs when the Antichrist goes into the rebuilt Temple in Israel three and a half years into the Tribulation and declares himself "God". Jesus also describes the Second Coming in detail. So, if the final generation began in 1948 and all end times events including the seven year Tribulation and the Second coming are going to occur within an 80-year window, we have an interesting scenario to consider.

The Rapture takes place before the Tribulation. This means that after the Rapture occurs, there will be seven more years to follow within the generation to which Jesus referred. This means if the Rapture occurs right now and you add seven more years for the Tribulation, we are basically at the eighty year point now. Again, I'm not setting dates, and I don't want you to either. But I hope you can see from all of this the exciting times we are living in and why the subtitle of this book is *The End Is Here*!

I want to address one more issue from the text in Matthew chapter 24 where Jesus describes the Second Coming and a gathering of saints with a trumpet blast by the angels "from the four winds, from one end of heaven to the other" (v. 31). Many well-intentioned people who believe we will live through the Tribulation are confused by this passage and believe this is the Rapture of the Church. But it isn't. The Rapture of the Church, which Jesus graphically describes in Luke chapter 17, occurs just before the Tribulation begins.

The Rapture Jesus describes in Matthew chapter 24 is for those who have been saved during the Tribulation. There will be many millions (if not billions) of believers on the earth when the Second Coming occurs. Some will be alive, and some will have been martyred. Here is a passage from Revelation chapter 20 that describes what happens to the tribulation saints who have been martyred:

> And I saw thrones, and they sat on them, and judgment was committed to them. Then *I saw* the souls of those who had been beheaded for their witness to Jesus and for the word of God, who had not worshiped the beast or his image, and had not received *his* mark on their foreheads or on their hands. And they lived and reigned with Christ for a thousand years. But the rest of the dead did not live again until the thousand years were finished. This *is* the first resurrection. Blessed and holy *is* he who has part in the first resurrection. Over such the second death has no power, but they shall be priests of God and of Christ, and shall reign with Him a thousand years (Revelation 20:4–6).

This passage is describing what is happening when we return with Jesus at the Second Coming (described in detail in Revelation chapter 19). Not only are living believers raptured from around the world as Jesus described in Matthew chapter 24, but these brave martyrs that have been killed for their refusal to receive the mark of the beast and to worship him are raptured to join the already raptured church as the triumphant wife of Jesus Christ. As we have been with Jesus for seven years in heaven for the marriage supper of the Lamb, they have had to endure the Tribulation. The reason for this is because when the Rapture of the Church occurred, they weren't believers at that time.

I hope this chapter helps you to understand where we are in relation to God's prophetic clock. Without a doubt, I believe we are the final generation living in the end of the end times. But I don't believe we should stop living or stop making plans for the future. Here is what I tell people all of the time: plan like Jesus isn't coming back for 100 years but live like He is coming back today! This is how I live my life, and I encourage you to do the same.

PLAN LIKE JESUS ISN'T
COMING BACK FOR 100 YEARS
BUT LIVE LIKE HE IS COMING
BACK TODAY!

Noah and Lot proclaimed righteousness and exemplified godly living in evil times. In our day, God is calling us to do likewise. Your faith is not a source of shame or fear; it is what makes you bold. Jesus said, "Whoever is ashamed of Me and My words in this adulterous and sinful generation, of him the Son of Man also will be ashamed when He comes in the glory of His Father with the holy angels" (Mark 8:38). I'm not ashamed of Jesus Christ nor the Holy Spirit. I'm not embarrassed about the Word of God. I'm not uncomfortable with Scripture's standards. The only thing for which I can confess shame is the way I lived before I turned my life completely over to Jesus.

Don't envy sinners or be deceived by them. Shortly before the Flood, arrogant and ungodly people strutted around and acted as if nothing bad would ever happen to them. There would be no end to business as usual. They could get away with anything, and no one would stand against them. They especially did not expect God's opposition. In their eyes Noah was stupid and crazy. Then Noah went into the ark with his family, and God shut the door. When the rain started I'm sure Noah could hear people pounding on the door, pleading for him to open it.

Before the Flood the earth had never needed nor experienced rain. Yet there was Noah, building a massive ship in the middle of dry ground. Imagine the mockery he must have endured. Every time somebody saw that ship, it was one more opportunity to roast Noah with another joke. But then the Flood began, and Noah looked like the smartest man in the world.

Some of you have been mocked for your faith. Your family or friends may be laughing at you, even as you read this book. They may think you are weird because you believe in Jesus and His return. But on the day after the Rapture, you too will look like a genius. My prayer is that they won't be on the outside pleading to get in after it is too late.

The angels came to rescue Lot and his family. Then the arrogant and ungodly men of the city tried to force themselves sexually on the angels (I can't think of anything much worse). Those people had no fear of God at all. So God took Lot and his family out, and then fire and brimstone fell. Think about the next day, when the cities of Sodom and Gomorrah were smoldering ruins of ash. If anyone in the surrounding towns survived, what do you think they would have had to say about Lot then?

I was in New York City after 9/11. Before I continue, I want to clarify that I am *not* saying this tragedy was because of the judgment of God. I'm only illustrating the difference of before and after. New York is normally full of noise, character, and frantic business, but that was not the case right after 9/11. No, it was chillingly quiet. People were polite and respectful. Automobile horns were silent. There was a noticeable humility on the people of the city. I must tell you that the Tribulation will make 9/11 seem as mild as a Sunday school party. The world will change dramatically the day after the Rapture. Again, don't envy sinners. They will be severely judged by God very soon.

Psalm 2 is an incredibly important prophecy of the end times. It speaks of a time when the world will rebel against "the Lord and against His Anointed" (v. 2). That is the Psalmist's way of saying God the Father and His Son Jesus. In this passage, God responds to the world's attempts to reject His authority.

Why do the nations rage,
And the people plot a vain thing?
The kings of the earth set themselves,
And the rulers take counsel together,
Against the LORD and against His Anointed, *saying,*
"Let us break Their bonds in pieces
And cast away Their cords from us."
He who sits in the heavens shall laugh;
The Lord shall hold them in derision.
Then He shall speak to them in His wrath,
And distress them in His deep displeasure:
"Yet I have set My King
On My holy hill of Zion."
"I will declare the decree:
The LORD has said to Me,
'You *are* My Son,
Today I have begotten You.
Ask of Me, and I will give *You*
The nations *for* Your inheritance,

And the ends of the earth *for* Your possession.
You shall break them with a rod of iron;
You shall dash them to pieces like a potter's vessel.'"
Now therefore, be wise, O kings;
Be instructed, you judges of the earth.
Serve the LORD with fear,
And rejoice with trembling.
Kiss the Son, lest He be angry,
And you perish *in* the way,
When His wrath is kindled but a little.
Blessed *are* all those who put their trust in Him (Psalm 2:1–12).

This passage vividly describes what is happening around the world right now. We are witnessing an unprecedented rebellion against God and His Word. The presence of the Antichrist spirit is palpable. As the nations rage against God's authority, He sits in heaven laughing at them. Watching the world try to defy God's authority is like watching a group of two-year olds plotting to take over the house. Psalm chapter 2 is a very comforting passage that reminds us that God is still in control and He knew all of this was coming.

Take special note of the final verse in this Psalm:

Kiss the Son, lest He be angry,
And you perish *in* the way,
When His wrath is kindled but a little.
Blessed *are* all those who put their trust in Him (2:12).

God is speaking about the end times and giving a warning to the leaders of the earth. If they will not "kiss the Son" (meaning

Jesus) and bow down to Him, then He will visit them in His wrath. The apostle John wrote this about the Tribulation at the end of human history:

> And the kings of the earth, the great men, the rich men, the commanders, the mighty men, every slave and every free man, hid themselves in the caves and in the rocks of the mountains, and said to the mountains and rocks, "Fall on us and hide us from the face of Him who sits on the throne and from the wrath of the Lamb! For the great day of His wrath has come, and who is able to stand?" (Revelation 6:15–17).

These kings and great men of the earth are the same group of people God was addressing in Psalm chapter 2. As they raged against the Lord and refused His authority, He warned them of the calamity that would fall on them. Then in Revelation chapter 6, the judgment is happening, and they are crying out for the rocks to fall on them to hide them from the Lamb. Even though they are hoping it will end quickly, it is some very bad news for them. John tells how desperate they will be: "In those days men will seek death and will not find it; they will desire to die, and death will flee from them" (Revelation 9:6).

We cannot imagine a worse fate. The people described in these passages will be living in the worst seven years of all human history, and God will supernaturally prevent many of them from dying or committing suicide. This event will be God's punishment upon them for refusing to acknowledge Jesus Christ as Lord and receive His salvation as an act of grace.

Nevertheless, I will not close this book on such a tragic note. This is the good news: If you are a believer and have "kissed the Son," then this will not be your experience. You won't face the days of wrath. Rather, as unbelievers are being judged for their rebellion here on earth, you will be receiving your eternal reward in the presence of God at the Father's House. During the seven-year Tribulation when God's wrath falls here on earth, the Church is in heaven marrying Jesus in the greatest matrimonial celebration the universe has ever known.

Today as you observe the ways people are behaving, it might seem that we are at a disadvantage as Christians. In fact, you may even be persecuted for your political, moral, or theological beliefs. But I urge you to open your eyes to the eternal perspective. You must not envy or follow those who are in rebellion against God. Remember the warnings of Psalm chapter 2 and Revelation chapters 6 and 9. We are still in the age of grace— God is still patiently offering every person an opportunity to "kiss His Son." Very soon, however, we as believers will be raptured to be with the Lord. Then the wrath of the Lamb will punish those who thought they could cast God aside.

Finally, I leave you with this: live for God, not this world. Put Jesus first, whatever it takes. Surround yourself with other believers who will support you and help you to be accountable. The writer of Hebrews says, "Let us consider one another in order to stir up love and good works, not forsaking the assembling of ourselves together, as *is* the manner of some, but exhorting *one another*, and so much the more as you see the Day approaching" (Hebrews 10:24–25).

I have known Jesus for almost five decades. I accepted Him as my Lord and Savior a week before I married Karen. I'm a pastor and a committed student of the Bible. However, if I neglected Christian fellowship, I am sure I would fall. I don't know how I would fall, but I know I would not live for Christ like I do today. I need close Christian friends around me who will hold me accountable. I don't think you can make it without godly friends and the Church. Your future will be shaped by the people with whom you surround yourself.

A wolf never attacks close to the shepherd or in the middle of the flock. He wants to get a single sheep alone. Likewise, the devil is always looking for lone Christians wandering on their own. Don't let him get you alone so he can take advantage of you. Make this commitment today: *I am committed to finding a Bible-based church and being an active member in fellowship with other believers. And until Jesus comes, nothing is going to take me out.* Then live by it. You will be successful as a follower of Jesus and ready for His return.

You might wonder why it is so important for Christians to live righteous lives if the world is going to get so bad anyway. Why is it important for you to minister to your family, work diligently in your job, contribute generously to your church with your time and finances, and vote righteously when the time comes to cast your ballot? What difference will it make if Jesus is coming and the world becomes even worse in the meantime? The difference it will make is *you!*

You will give a witness to the Light in the middle of the darkness. You will have no reason to be ashamed when you see Jesus face-to-face. You will become more like Him. You will draw others into the ark before the door is shut. And when He comes, you will be ready. In the words of Abraham Davenport, let candles be brought and let us be found doing our duty.

One more thing: if you know you haven't received Christ into your heart as your Lord and Savior or if you aren't sure, read the Appendix that follows this chapter. I will lead you in a prayer to receive Christ and give you some important instructions.

RECEIVING CHRIST & FIRST STEPS

SALVATION

We all need to be saved or "born again" because we are born spiritually dead. The reason for this is Adam and Eve's sin in the Garden of Eden. They were created by God as living physical and spiritual beings. But God warned them that if they ate the forbidden fruit, they would die. And they did!

The instant they ate the fruit, they died spiritually and fell morally. And they have passed their condition on to all of us. The only answer is to receive Jesus so our spirits can be reborn. Consider the following passage of Scripture:

There was a man of the Pharisees named Nicodemus, a ruler of the Jews. This man came to Jesus by night and said to Him, "Rabbi, we know that You are a teacher come from God; for no one can do these signs that You do unless God is with him."

Jesus answered and said to him, "Most assuredly, I say to you, unless one is born again, he cannot see the kingdom of God."

Nicodemus said to Him, "How can a man be born when he is old? Can he enter a second time into his mother's womb and be born?"

Jesus answered, "Most assuredly, I say to you, unless one is born of water and the Spirit, he cannot enter the kingdom of God. That which is born of the flesh is flesh, and that which is born of the Spirit is spirit. Do not marvel that I said to you, 'You must be born again.' The wind blows where it wishes, and you hear the sound of it, but cannot tell where it comes from and where it goes. So is everyone who is born of the Spirit."

Nicodemus answered and said to Him, "How can these things be?" (John 3:1–9).

When we open our hearts to Jesus and ask Him to come into our lives, we are born again as the Holy Spirit comes into us and regenerates our dead spirits. This means several things:

1. We are forgiven of our sins as we repent of rebellion to God and submit to His authority as Lord of our lives.

2. We are given the gift of eternal life and will live forever in heaven with Jesus.

3. We are now fully alive spiritual beings, capable of a personal relationship with Jesus. We can talk to Him in a personal manner in prayer, and we can hear His voice with our spiritual ears.

If you are ready to pray to receive Christ, pray this prayer:

Lord Jesus, I repent of my sins and rebellion against Your authority. I receive You into my heart as my Lord and Savior. I also receive Your blood on the cross as the payment for all of my sins and believe I'm totally forgiven by You. Thank You for the free gifts of forgiveness and eternal life. Fill me with Your Holy Spirit and give me the power to change and follow You all the days of my life. In Jesus' name, Amen.

If you prayed that prayer and truly meant it, then congratulations! You are now a Christian, and Christ is in your heart. I prayed a prayer similar to that almost 50 years ago, and it revolutionized my life. But it all happened one day at a time as I sought the Lord and grew as a believer. Here are some important steps to take in your new life as a believer:

WATER BAPTISM

You need to be water baptized. It is extremely important in your life as a Christian. Here is what Jesus said about it:

> Go into all the world and preach the gospel to every creature. **He who believes and is baptized will be saved**; but he who does not believe will be condemned (Mark 16:15–16, emphasis added).

As I stated earlier in the book, water baptism is the covenant seal of the New Covenant. In other words, it seals the deal. At your earliest convenience you need to go to your church, tell them what you have done in receiving Jesus, and ask them to water baptize you. If you don't have a church or if your church doesn't baptize in water, you need to find a Bible-believing church that will baptize you. Don't put it off. This is your first important step of obedience as a new believer, and it is a critical one.

God does a supernatural work in our hearts when we are water baptized. Here is what the apostle Paul tells us about this:

> In Him you were also circumcised with the circumcision made without hands, by putting off the body of the sins of the flesh, by the circumcision of Christ, buried with Him in baptism, in which you also were raised with *Him* through faith in the working of God, who raised Him from the dead (Colossians 2:11–12).

Water baptism is called "the circumcision of Christ." Circumcision was the seal of the covenant between God and the people of Israel (Genesis 17:10–11). If a Jewish man was not circumcised, then he was living outside the covenant. Likewise, water baptism is the seal of the covenant between Christ and believers. It is our first public step of obedience and shows our good faith in making Jesus the Lord of our lives. Without being water baptized you will never have the same level of confidence about your standing with the Lord, and you won't experience the supernatural miracle that happens in your heart through baptism.

There is another powerful reason to be water baptized. Without being too graphic, circumcision relates to a male penis. When a baby boy is born, he has excess skin on his penis that covers the tip. If that skin isn't removed, issues with hygiene and sexual sensitivity can later arise. Likewise, a believer who hasn't been water baptized struggles more with sin or "spiritual hygiene" and lacks sensitivity to the Lord, thereby stunting his or her spiritual capacity to relate to Jesus in an intimate manner. As you can see, water baptism is a big deal, and you need to do it as quickly as possible.

No one can make the decision for you to be saved and baptized other than you. It's nice for parents to dedicate their children to God, but the decision of salvation is for each individual to decide. The same is true for water baptism. You may have previously been baptized as a baby or at another time, but according to the Bible, the correct order is salvation and then baptism.

Finally, in being baptized you are making a public profession of your faith in Christ, and that is powerful. It is so important to tell someone what you have done, and nothing could do that better than being baptized. Also, when you stand up for Jesus and are water baptized, it encourages others to do the same. I have never seen a person who lived a significant life for the Lord who wasn't water baptized.

THE BIBLE

You need to get a Bible that you can read and understand. There are some electronic Bibles found on sites and apps such as BibleGateway.com and YouVersion. These allow you to select from many different translations. I personally use the New King James Version, but I also recommend the New Living Translation. If you would like to have a print copy of the Bible, I recommend the *Fresh Start Bible*. It is the New Living Translation, and in addition to the biblical text, it also contains many helpful discipleship tools written by myself and other trusted Christian leaders.

It is very important to develop a habit of reading your Bible every day. I use a daily reading plan on BibleGateway.com that takes me through the Bible in a year by reading for about 20 minutes each day. It is very helpful.

PRAYER

You need to make a daily habit of prayer. This is a time where you take your needs, desires, hurts, and burdens to the Lord and ask Him for help and direction. I wrote a book called *Ten Steps Toward Christ* for the purpose of helping new believers learn to pray, read the Bible, hear God's voice, and other important steps. I encourage you to buy it and read it. It will guide you through many important steps in your new life in Christ. You can find it on marriagetoday.com or Amazon.com.

CHURCH

You need to be a committed member in a strong, Bible-believing church. If you don't have a church already, you might need to visit a number of churches before finding one you like. We live in a very evil age, and we need people around us to encourage us in our faith and to hold us accountable.

After I became a believer at 19 years old, my wife and I joined a church and got involved. Besides accepting Christ, that was the best thing we ever did. It changed the course of our lives. It gave us critical support for our marriage and with our children. And we also learned about the Lord and how to fulfill the destiny He has for us. Truly, it has transformed our lives. All of our close friendships are with our church family, and they are the best friends in the world.

BAPTISM IN THE HOLY SPIRIT

Last but certainly not least, you need to ask the Lord to baptize you in the Holy Spirit. None of us have the power to change or serve the Lord without the Holy Spirit's help. There is an entire chapter on this in my book *Ten Steps Toward Christ*. I encourage you to read it.

The Holy Spirit is God, and He wants to walk with us through anything we are experiencing. Don't rely on your own strength. Baptism in the Holy Spirit is a free gift available to every follower of Christ. He will give you strength to serve the Lord and live as you should.

Again, congratulations on receiving Jesus as your Lord and Savior. May the Lord bless you!

ABOUT THE AUTHOR

Jimmy Evans is senior pastor of Gateway Church in the Dallas/ Fort Worth Metroplex. He is also the founder and CEO of MarriageToday. Jimmy has studied end times prophecy for more than 45 years and has taught it worldwide to millions of people. He is passionate about helping believers find hope, peace, and encouragement in the Word of God. Jimmy has authored more than seventeen books including *Marriage on the Rock, The Overcoming Life, The Four Laws of Love,* and *I Am David.* Jimmy and Karen have been married for 47 years and have two married children and five grandchildren.

NOTES

Introduction

1. Malcolm Gladwell, *The Tipping Point: How Little Things Can Make a Big Difference* (Boston, MA: Little, Brown and Company, 2000), 12.

Chapter Two

2. The Editors of Encyclopaedia Britannica. "Balfour Declaration," Encyclopædia Britannica (Encyclopædia Britannica, inc., October 26, 2019), https://www.britannica.com/event/Balfour-Declaration.

3. "Franklin Roosevelt Administration: Letter to King of Saudi Arabia Regarding Palestine," President Roosevelt Letter to King of Saudi Arabia Regarding Palestine (April 1945) accessed December 20, 2019, https://www.jewishvirtuallibrary.org/president-roosevelt-letter-to-king-of-saudi-arabia-regarding-palestine-april-1945.

4. "British Palestine Mandate: History & Overview." History & Overview of the British Palestine Mandate, accessed December 20, 2019, https://www.jewishvirtuallibrary.org/history-and-overview-of-the-british-palestine-mandate.

5. "Creation of Israel, 1948," U.S. Department of State, accessed December 20, 2019, https://history.state.gov/milestones/1945-1952/creation-israel.

6. "Creation of Israel, 1948."

7. Jon Huntzinger, "Joshua," in *Fresh Start Bible*, ed. John Andersen and Jenny Morgan (Southlake: Gateway Press, 2019), 185.

8. "The U.N. and Israel: Key Statistics from UN Watch," UN Watch, October 5, 2019, https://unwatch.org/un-israel-key-statistics.

9. "ESCWA Launches Report on Israeli Practices Towards the Palestinian People and the Question of Apartheid," United Nations Economic and Social Commission for Western Asia, March 15, 2017, https://www.unescwa.org/news/escwa-launches-report-israeli-practices-towards-palestinian-people-and-question-apartheid.

10. "General Assembly Asserts Land-For-Peace Principle Is Still Key to Settlement of Question of Palestine | Meetings Coverage and Press Releases," (United Nations, December 2, 1998), https://www.un.org/press/en/1998/19981202.ga9522.html.

11. World Jewish Congress, "Israeli Rabbi Says Katrina Was Punishment For Gaza Withdrawal," World Jewish Congress, September 8. 2005, https://www.worldjewishcongress.org/en/news/israeli-rabbi-says-katrina-was-punishment-for-gaza-withdrawal.

12. "Negotiated Two-State Solution Still 'the Only Option' for Palestine: Guterres | UN News," (United Nations, November 28, 2018), https://news.un.org/en/story/2018/11/1026871.

13. The Covenant Of The Hamas - Main Points, accessed December 21, 2019, https://fas.org/irp/world/para/docs/880818a.htm.

14. "President Donald J. Trump Keeps His Promise To Open U.S. Embassy In Jerusalem, Israel," The White House (The United States Government, May 14, 2018), https://www.whitehouse.gov/briefings-statements/president-donald-j-trump-keeps-promise-open-u-s-embassy-jerusalem-israel.

15. Michael Schwirtz and Rick Gladstone, "U.S. Vetoes U.N. Resolution Condemning Move on Jerusalem," (The New York Times, December 18, 2017), https://www.nytimes.com/2017/12/18/world/middleeast/jerusalem-un-security-council.html.

16. Jessica Durando and Oren Dorell, "Here Are the 7 Small Nations That Sided with U.S. and Israel on U.N.'s Jerusalem Vote," USA Today (Gannett Satellite Information Network, December 21, 2017), https://www.usatoday.com/story/news/world/2017/12/21/here-7-nations-sided-u-s-and-israel-u-n-vote-over-jerusalem/974098001.

17. Ali Sawafta, "Palestinians Angry at Reports of Early U.S. Embassy Move to Jerusalem," Reuters (Thomson Reuters, February 24, 2018), https://www.reuters.com/article/us-usa-israel-palestinians/palestinians-angry-at-reports-of-early-u-s-embassy-move-to-jerusalem-idUSKCN1G72B3.

18. "U.S. Embassy Moves to Jerusalem," USA Today (Gannett Satellite Information Network, May 14, 2018), https://www.usatoday.com/picture-gallery/news/world/2018/05/13/us-embassy-moves-to-jerusalem/34873575.

19. Bill Chappell, "55 Palestinian Protesters Killed, Gaza Officials Say, As U.S.

Opens Jerusalem Embassy," (NPR, May 14, 2018), https://www.npr.org/sections/thetwo-way/2018/05/14/610934534/18-palestinian-protesters-die-gaza-officials-say-as-u-s-opens-jerusalem-embassy.

20. "The Last Blood Moon," Jewish Voice Ministries International, September 24, 2015, https://www.jewishvoice.org/read/blog/the-last-blood-moon-days-away.

21. "1967: The Reunification of Jerusalem," mfa.gov.il, accessed December 21, 2019, https://mfa.gov.il/Jubilee-years/Pages/1967-The-Reunification-of-Jerusalem.aspx.

22. "Catalog of Lunar Eclipses: 1901 to 2000".

23. "Catalog of Lunar Eclipses: 2001 to 2100".

24. Kate Lohnes, "Siege of Jerusalem," Encyclopædia Britannica (Encyclopædia Britannica, inc., November 13, 2019), https://www.britannica.com/event/Siege-of-Jerusalem-70.

Chapter Three

25. "Iran, Russia Start Construction of New Iranian Nuclear Plant," Reuters (Thomson Reuters, September 10, 2016), https://www.reuters.com/article/us-iran-russia-nuclearpower-idUSKCN11G0EB.

26. Michael Crowley, "The Iran Crisis, Explained," (The New York Times, June 17, 2019), https://www.nytimes.com/2019/06/17/us/politics/iran-nuclear-deal-uranium.html.

27. Jayson Casper, "Who Awaits the Messiah Most? Muslims," ChristianityToday.com (Christianity Today, December 17, 2019), https://www.christianity-today.com/ct/2017/january-february/who-awaits-messiah-most-muslims-isis-dabiq-eschatology.html.

28. Thomas Erdbrink, "U.S. Remains the 'Great Satan,' Hard-Liners in Iran Say," (The New York Times, September 1, 2015), https://www.nytimes.com/2015/09/02/world/middleeast/us-remains-the-great-satan-hard-liners-in-iran-say.html.

29. Kate Cooch, "Operation Babylon: Israel's Strike on Al-Tuwaitha," Warfare History Network, May 5, 2017, https://warfarehistorynetwork.com/2017/05/04/operation-babylon-israels-strike-on-al-tuwaitha.

30. Ian Bremmer, "Syria's Civil War Complicated By Multiple Proxy Battles," (Time, February 16, 2018), https://time.com/5162409/syria-civil-war-proxy-battles.

31. Jeffrey Scott Shapiro, "Administration Denies Obama Threatened to Shoot down Israeli Warplanes," (The Washington Times, March 1, 2015), https://www.washingtontimes.com/news/2015/mar/1/report-obama-threatened-shoot-down-israeli-warplan.

32. "Iran Nuclear Deal: Enriched Uranium Limit Will Be Breached on 27 June," BBC News (BBC, June 17, 2019), https://www.bbc.com/news/world-middle-east-48661843.

33. Doreen Horschig, "Israel Could Strike First as Tensions with Iran Flare," Public Radio International, June 21, 2019, https://www.pri.org/stories/2019-06-21/israel-could-strike-first-tensions-iran-flare.

34. Gerald Steinberg, "The Begin Doctrine at 25," The Jerusalem Post | JPost.com, June 4, 2006, https://www.jpost.com/Features/The-Begin-Doctrine-at-25.

35. Doreen Horschig, "Israel Could Strike First as Tensions with Iran Flare".

36. Alexei Anishchuk, "Russia Warns Israel Not to Attack Iran," Reuters (Thomson Reuters, February 22, 2012), https://www.reuters.com/article/us-iran-russia-idUSTRE81L0SR20120222.

37. Jeremy Sharon, "Jewish Prayer Has Returned to the Temple Mount - Exclusive," The Jerusalem Post, December 12, 2019, https://www.jpost.com/Arab-Israeli-Conflict/Jewish-prayer-has-returned-to-the-Temple-Mount-exclusive-610781.

38. Atara Beck, "Temple Institute: We Are Preparing to Rebuild the Holy Temple," UWI, July 3, 2017, https://unitedwithisrael.org/temple-institute-preparing-to-rebuild-the-holy-temple.

Chapter Four

39. Molly Billings, "The Influenza Pandemic of 1918," June 1997, https://virus.stanford.edu/uda/.

40. Fred Espenak, "Total Solar Eclipse of -1776 Nov 30," EclipseWise, May 19, 2016, http://www.eclipsewise.com/solar/SEgmap/-1799--1700/SE-1776Nov30Tgmap.html.

41. Reitz North America, "29 FACTS about Today's Eclipse: Solar Eclipse," Industrial Fans and Blowers - Blog, July 21, 2017, https://www.reitznorthamerica.com/29-facts-about-todays-eclipse.

42. "History of Aransas - Aransas," U.S. Fish & Wildlife Service, February 5, 2019, https://www.fws.gov/refuge/Aransas/about/history/aransas.html.

43. D. M. Murdock, "The Star in the East and Three Kings," Stellar House Publishing, December 10, 2019, https://stellarhousepublishing.com/star-east-three-kings/. Excerpted and adapted from *Christ in Egypt: The Horus-Jesus Connection* (Seattle, WA: Stellar House Publishing, LLC, 2009).

44. Luis B. Vega, "#361: REVELATION 12 SIGN COMPOSITE," PostScripts, accessed March 10, 2020, https://www.postscripts.org/ps-news-361.html.

Chapter Five

45. "Facts and Case Summary - Engel v. Vitale," United States Courts, accessed December 27, 2019, https://www.uscourts.gov/educational-resources/educational-activities/facts-and-case-summary-engel-v-vitale.

46. Stephen R. McCullough, "School District of Abington Township v. Schempp," Encyclopædia Britannica (Encyclopædia Britannica, inc., June 10, 2019), https://www.britannica.com/topic/School-District-of-Abington-Township-v-Schempp.

47. Berkley Center for Religion and Georgetown University, "Stone v. Graham," Berkley Center for Religion, Peace and World Affairs, accessed December 27, 2019, https://berkleycenter.georgetown.edu/cases/stone-v-graham.

48. Larry Shannon-Missal, "Americans' Belief in God, Miracles and Heaven Declines," The Harris Poll, December 16, 2013, https://theharrispoll.com/new-york-n-y-december-16-2013-a-new-harris-poll-finds-that-while-a-strong-majority-74-of-u-s-adults-do-believe-in-god-this-belief-is-in-decline-when-compared-to-previous-years-as-just-over.

49. "America's Changing Religious Landscape," Pew Research Center's Religion & Public Life Project, May 12, 2015, https://www.pewforum.org/2015/05/12/americas-changing-religious-landscape.

50. "America's Changing Religious Landscape".

51. Michael Shermer, "The Number of Americans with No Religious Affiliation Is Rising," Scientific American (Scientific American, April 1, 2018), https://

www.scientificamerican.com/article/the-number-of-americans-with-no-religious-affiliation-is-rising.

52. The Editors of Encyclopaedia Britannica, "Obergefell v. Hodges," Encyclopædia Britannica (Encyclopædia Britannica, inc., August 23, 2019), https://www.britannica.com/event/Obergefell-v-Hodges.

Chapter Seven

53. Walt Heyer, "Transgender Regret Is Real Even If The Media Says Otherwise," The Federalist, August 19, 2015, https://thefederalist.com/2015/08/19/transgender-regret-is-real-even-if-the-media-tell-you-otherwise/.

Chapter Eight

54. Marc Rosenberg, "Marc My Words: The Coming Knowledge Tsunami," Learning Solutions Magazine, October 10, 2017, https://learningsolutionsmag.com/articles/2468/marc-my-words-the-coming-knowledge-tsunami.

55. "U.S. Patent Statistics Chart Calendar Years 1963 - 2018," U.S. Patent Statistics Summary Table, Calendar Years 1963 to 2018, 04/2019 update, accessed January 3, 2020, https://www.uspto.gov/web/offices/ac/ido/oeip/taf/us_stat.htm.

56. J. Halamka et al., "The Security Implications of VeriChip Cloning," *Journal of the American Medical Informatics Association*13, no. 6 (2006): pp. 601-607, https://doi.org/10.1197/jamia.m2143.

57. *Jurassic Park*, directed by Stephen Spielberg (1993; Universal City, CA: Universal Pictures, 2000), DVD.

58. "Human Genetic Modification," Human Genetic Modification | Center for Genetics and Society, accessed January 3, 2020, https://www.geneticsandsociety.org/topics/human-genetic-modification.

59. "Human Genetic Modification".

60. David DiSalo, "The Era Of Genetically-Altered Humans Could Begin This Year," Forbes (Forbes Magazine, January 26, 2014), https://www.forbes.com/sites/daviddisalvo/2014/01/26/the-era-of-genetically-altered-humans-could-begin-this-year/#2bdb300d9df3.

61. "Human Genetic Modification".

62. Julia Hollingsworth and Isaac Yee, "Chinese Gene-Editing Scientist Jailed for 3 Years," CNN (Cable News Network, December 30, 2019), https://www.cnn.com/2019/12/30/china/gene-scientist-china-intl-hnk/index.html.

63. Samantha Masunaga, "Lawsuit over Quarter Horse's Clone May Redefine Animal Breeding," (Los Angeles Times, March 14, 2015), https://www.latimes.com/nation/la-na-cloned-horses-20150314-story.html.

64. Robert Johnson, "British Scientists Have Secretly Created More Than 150 Human-Animal Hybrids," (Business Insider, July 23, 2011), https://www.businessinsider.com/scientists-creating-human-animal-hybrid-embryos-2011-7.

65. David Cyranoski, "Japan Approves First Human-Animal Embryo Experiments," Nature News (Nature Publishing Group, July 26, 2019), https://www.nature.com/articles/d41586-019-02275-3.

66. Jillian Eugenios, "Ray Kurzweil: Humans Will Be Hybrids by 2030," CNNMoney (Cable News Network, June 4, 2015), https://money.cnn.com/2015/06/03/technology/ray-kurzweil-predictions/index.html.

67. Zoltan Istvan, "Singularity or Transhumanism: What Word Should We Use to Discuss the Future?," Slate Magazine (Slate, August 28, 2014), https://slate.com/technology/2014/08/singularity-transhumanism-humanity-what-word-should-we-use-to-discuss-the-future.html.

Chapter Ten

68. Evan Andrews, "Remembering New England's 'Dark Day,'" History.com (A&E Television Networks, August 22, 2018), https://www.history.com/news/remembering-new-englands-dark-day.

69. "TorahCalendar.com," accessed January 6, 2020, https://torahcalendar.com.

The Tipping Point Prophecy Update

by Jimmy Evans

In this timely email newsletter, Jimmy Evans draws on decades of study, experience and biblical expertise as he explains the striking parallels between current world events and the prophecies of Scripture.

Subscribe to this newsletter for just $7/month. You'll get insightful emails every week, exclusive access to podcast episodes and much more.

ENDTIMES.COM

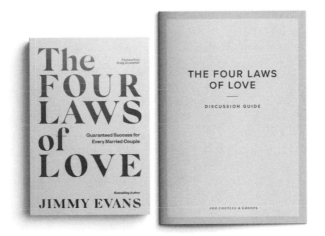